PLINY STEELE BOYD

UP AND DOWN THE MERRIMAC,

A Vacation Trip

BY

PLINY STEELE BOYD

SicPress 2013
Methuen, Mass.

Up and Down the Merrimac: A Vacation Trip was originally published in 1879 at Boston by Lothrop

to John G. Whittier,
"Whose verse has given him a claim on the Merrimac, from the white hills to the sea, this attempt on the part of one of his friends and neighbors to grind a small grist at his winter privilege is respectfully inscribed."

©2013
SicPress.com
14 Pleasant St.
Methuen, Massachusetts.
sales@sicpress.com

TABLE OF CONTENTS

UP THE MERRIMAC

Chapter I. Preliminary. 7
Chapter II. the start. 10
Chapter III. Rowing with the Tide. 15
Chapter IV. a Thunder-storm. 20
Chapter V. the Broken Oar. 25
Chapter VI. our First Sunday. 31
Chapter VII. Onward and Upward. 36
Chapter VIII. Rowing up-Stairs. 42
Chapter IX. Passaconaway Island. 45
Chapter X. Looking Toward Sunrise. 51
Chapter XI. Solitude and Society. 56

DOWN THE MERRIMAC

Chapter XII. Homeward Bound. 63
Chapter XIII. a Pinch of Salt. 68
Chapter XIV. the New Earth. 72
Chapter XV. Our Last Sunday. 78
Chapter XVI. Music in the Air. 83
Chapter XVII. Home Again. 88
Authors Biography 97

Up the Merrimac
Chapter I: Preliminary.

It was a happy thought that crept into the brain of Columbus when he determined to discover America.

Just how the thought was evolved, precisely when and where, has not been handed down to us. By what combination of material elements the thought was produced, remains yet to be discovered.

We do not know what he ate for breakfast that morning. And if we knew, we could not affirm with certainty, whether it was the fish, or the fowl that laid the egg, that hatched the thought of America. It may be evidence of the backwardness of our age that we are not able to determine exactly how to combine the products of the soil so as to originate great thoughts. That is one of the discoveries for some future Columbus of mental or material philosophers. Let us not make haste to rob him of his glory. It will be considerate to leave to posterity a few of the great inventions yet to be made. When it comes our turn to interview the great Edison, we shall modestly caution him against loading down the present century with too many brilliant inventions.

But so fruitful of good was that little venture of the great explorer, that we have often wondered there were not more Columbuses in the world.

"*Lives of great men all remind us*"—

It was not with any idea of making our lives sublime, however, that we determined to make a voyage of discovery up the Merrimac.

But all perilous adventures have a certain fascination about them. And spite of our high-wrought civilization, there is considerable of the gypsy left in us yet. And to gratify the gypsy, as well as to enjoy the luxury of discovery, and the fascination of peril, we took for our vacation trip a row and sail up the Merrimac—myself and two boys. It would be a work of supererogation to assign all the reasons for choosing the Merrimac rather than the Atlantic for our explorations. It will suffice to state that our time, our purse, and our ship were all too short for an ocean voyage.

And, moreover, the navigator whose ambition can be curbed within the limits of the Merrimac, can the more easily go ashore nights. And in case of being upset, or spilled overboard, he can the more easily touch bottom. But our ambition to make discoveries did not run so much in a perpendicular direction, as horizontally. And the horizons of the Atlantic, after reaching mid-ocean, are tame compared with the picturesque shores of our river. So up river we determined to go.

And for fear some wretched historian would make a botch of the story, it has seemed good for me to tell it myself.

There is a great advantage in being the historian of your own adventures; for then you can be sure of telling the truth. All you have to do is to follow the facts. But the historian of others' adventures has to rely too largely upon his imagination; and the truth often suffers from the coloring it gets from the historian's fancy. When, however, you color it with your own fancy, you know just how much is truth, and how much is coloring. Of these records, the writer feels a strong assurance that the facts narrated are not purely imaginary. They are not facts founded on fiction. All the genuine facts were of actual occurrence. If any fictitious events are allowed to transpire in the narrative, they will be sufficiently indicated, and the reader duly cautioned against believing too much.

If the record seems to carry the semblance of a semi-romance, it is due either to the romantic character of the adventures, or to the innocent play of the writer's fancy while recording them. There would be a certain advantage in recording the facts and the fancies in separate chapters, as a possible aid to future historians; but it is not now so much our purpose to lighten their labors, as to obviate them altogether. The man who undertakes to write his autobiography should leave no supplementary work for the historian. Why should we do our work so as to leave the necessity for having it done over and over again? Yet how much of man's time is spent in revising and making improvements upon the work of his predecessors!

If this chapter were not so full of more valuable material, it would be appropriate here to repeat a saying which is often forgotten in practice. but which is just as true as though it were never forgotten, that "whatever is worth doing at all is worth doing well." And it is confidently believed that in the subsequent chapters, the facts and the fancies are so well intermingled that no future historian will need to meddle with them.

It is needless to say, perhaps, that the romance was not discernible in the prosy preparations, the gathering of provisions and furnishings for camping out, and the waiting for suitable weather after the time for starting, so much as in the high hopes and lively anticipations of fair winds for sailing and propitious currents for rowing.

The pleasures of anticipation were never more vividly realized. The tasks seen in prospective were easy of accomplishment. The horizons to be discovered were full of beauty; those actually seen, the terrific thunder storms, the roaring rapids, the contrary-minded fish, the willing mosquitoes, and queer birds, actually encountered, have a romance of their own, as pleasing as they were fascinating. But in the words of the novelist, let us not anticipate. If the reader's curiosity is wrought up as high as the writer's hopes and fears were again and again in the midst of perils unforeseen but encountered, this will suffice for preliminary. The record of the trip will open with the next chapter.

CHAPTER II: THE START.

If any one thinks it was an easy matter for Columbus to get started on his voyage of discovery, after he concluded to find America, let him read again the history of that adventurer's efforts to obtain the patronage of the authorities and the consent of Mrs. Columbus.

For nearly twenty years he wandered from city to city, and from capital to capital in quest of a patron. It is no part of our plan to encumber these records with the objections which he had to encounter at home, and elsewhere. But it can hardly be considered any betrayal of confidence if we simply mention that Mrs. Columbus was dead set against it. That is, she worried herself to death in less than ten years, for fear of his being drowned, or eaten by cannibals beyond the horizon, who might mistake him for a missionary. Why she could not cheerfully sacrifice herself and him too on the altar of science, the historian forgets to tell us. That would certainly have seemed quite as heroic, quite as sublime, as to fret herself to death in the vain endeavor to prevent the world's progress.

A certain grand cardinal was not so foolish. True, he thought the project savored strongly of heterodoxy, yet he approved it. Some of his fellow-ecclesiastics remonstrated, piled up Bible texts in opposition to the plan, quoted the great divines, and marshalled a great array of authorities to prove that America ought not to be discovered. But persuaded by another high dignitary in the Church, Queen Isabella concluded that it ought to be discovered; and after nearly a score of years from the time when he first entertained the project, one bright morning at eight o'clock, August 3d, Columbus weighed anchor, and cheered by the approval of his second wife, and the blessing of the reigning queen, set sail for the New World.

In our home the reigning queen is Mrs. Columbus herself. But she is not in all respects like the first Mrs. Columbus. The perils of the proposed voyage may have aroused a similar feeling of apprehension. The idea of treacherous winds and angry billows may have flitted through her mind. Perhaps she thought of the sharpness of sharks' teeth, of bears' claws, of the playful habits of the sturgeon, and the unfriendly disposition of the mosquito, but she was altogether too sensible to worry herself to death. And though the first announcement of the plan was not hailed with unbounded enthusiasm, and some objections were mildly canvassed, when with evident interest she began to bake pies for the trip, we were sure we should not be compelled to leave home without her blessing. And that was well. Since nothing lends greater zest to an enterprise than the hearty approval of the ruling powers.

The last few days preceding our trip were days of busy preparation. Hooks, lines, corks, and sinkers, but not enough to sink the ship, were carefully packed in boxes.

Parsons evidently thought that a voyage of discovery over any waters would be a total failure without an elaborate outfit of fishing tackle. Bags, baskets, and bundles accumulated as if by magic; and yet we were to have a very light outfit, so that we might easily lift our ship over difficult places.

We took a tent and all the desired equipment for camping out, and fortunately, as the weather turned, all the essentials for camping in.

Our lantern, oil-stove and rubber blankets proved valuable safe-guards against cold, darkness, and dampness. When the rain poured in torrents we were sufficiently reminded that the weather as well as the ground was somewhat damp. The two days before we started were rainy days. If they had not been, we should have started two days earlier. After waiting impatiently during that fraction of a century, we expected fair weather. But if the antediluvians in the days of Noah thought, after it had rained two days, that the resources of the clouds were about exhausted, they were soon made aware of their mistake. We found that the two rainy days were not designed as a prophecy of fair weather.

But then, were we not to set sail on the moist element? Were not our discoveries to be in part of water? To a mariner nothing is of greater importance. Heaven was kind to furnish a bountiful supply.

On the morning of August first there appeared such evident signs of clearing, that the boys found no difficulty in shouting the word "*go*"

And the little boys that were not going, consented to aid in the shouting. If ever boys were in earnest, Wendell, and Parsons proved themselves thoroughly so by the incredibly short time required for dressing, eating, and packing. Our dory lay in waiting at Boardman's wharf, on the Powow, which appeared at that poiakes takes its rise in the Salisbury Woollen Mills, whose huge piles of brick and mortar stood as silent sentinels on the hill-side; but whose cards and spindles were having a sadly prolonged vacation. It was eight o'clock as we pushed off, leaving all manner of good wishes for the friends left behind, and hoping they would be able to endure the sweets and comforts of home, while we self-denying mortals set forth to try our fortunes and seamanship on the perilous waters.

Here, perhaps, is as good a place as any to mention that the reigning Queen had given us not only her blessing, but also her consent to accompany us a little way. This was an unlooked for favor, which served to prolong the pleasures of parting beyond all expectation.

It has been wittily said that philosophers crossing the sea of life are more intent upon finding where they came from, than where they are going to. The oarsman is your true philosopher, and sits facing the past, content to back out as quickly as he can get out.

Nothing was more natural, then, than for us to take a farewell look at the young city, that sat like a queen on the hill-side fast receding from sight. Of all the towns in the valley, Amesbury is one of the most interesting. Her wheel factories and carriage shops, with their curious machinery, are a marvel of enterprise and ingenuity. For varied and attractive scenery the town takes rank with—but we would not appear to flatter any of the neighboring towns. We were convinced that it was as good a place as any to start from, even though it was our home. The mouth of the Merrimac had been suggested to us as an excellent starting place. That is where the river itself starts, when it undertakes to go up stream. We were inclined, however, to attribute that not so much to the excellence of the place as to the fearfulness of it. The river recoils with terror from the thought of being lost in the storm-vexed Atlantic, and rushes back to the protection of the hills. The alternate explanation is that the river is so charmed by the beauty of the lower part of the valley, that it flows back to get a second blessing before venturing out to sea. To have made that our starting place, would have given us a sail by some sweet islands, and a sight of the shabbiest side of our "sea-blown city," near the mouth; but then, we should have had first to get there, and would have missed our row down the Powow. That is a river not to be slighted. It deserves to be chanted in lyric verse by all the muses that haunt the neighboring hills. Ours, which is the muse of History, may perhaps be excused from attempting it in this connection. We think, on the whole, the Powow deserves rather better treatment than our muse would be able to give it.

It is a beautiful river for navigation. There are no rapids in it, below the Mills. True, when all crooked things are made straight, there will be some changes made in its course. But that is true also of the Merrimac; and of some crooked people we know, whose course is hardly satisfactory.

Winding about, amid the tall grass and rushes, from which flocks of birds, with occasionally a bobolink, kept rising to celebrate our coming, we made the two miles and a half to the mouth just in time to greet the incoming tide. We shot quickly under the arch that joins the Ferry Village with Salisbury Point, and found ourselves on the broad bosom of the Merrimac at a point which commands some of the finest scenery in the world:

"*Sweet fields arrayed in living green,*
And rivers of delight."

We could see the towers of Moulton Castle, which adorns the green hill on the south bank, and to which distance lends a rare enchantment; and far up river we could see the spire of the West Newbury Church, and the politico-astronomical watchtower on Pipe-stave hill. We could see the reflection of the north bank, with its long row of dwellings near the street, with their bright flower-gardens, loaded orchards, and grand old elms. We could see the bend in the river below us, where it sweeps to the south to find the right place to run under the chain-bridge, that quaint monument of some old-time genius, which, were we dabbling in prophecy instead of history, we should send down river loaded like a scape-goat with the sins of fast drivers. We shall considerately defer that matter a little, so as not to deprive the Queen of Deer Island of the means of crossing to her beloved Newburyport, described in her picturesque and glowing periods as hardly less beautiful than the New Jerusalem.

We could see the stone towers of Hawkswood, standing like a sentinel by the rocky pass in the river, above the draw-bridge. To the west of us we could see the fine new factory on the Amesbury bank, where they make the neatest and cheapest device for collecting poll-taxes ever yet brought to our knowledge. We could almost see the sun shining upon this bewitching scenery. And turning our boat up stream, surrounded by all these attractions, we could almost see our Paradise.

The reader will prefer an invitation to visit a scene so favored to a full description, be it ever so prosy.

Chapter III. Rowing with the Tide.

It seemed a pity to sail away from so much beauty. But remembering that this should be a life of self-denial, in heroic mood we flung our sheet to the wind, determined to forego the pleasure of gazing longer.

The breeze did not seem to be inclined to reward that kind of self-denial. Æolus was faint-hearted. Was it out of pity for our supposed verdancy? Did he mean to suggest that it would be safer for us to row? Perhaps he was out of wind, and had not learned our modern methods of raising it. We did not wait to consult the oracles. We did not wish to disappoint the tide that had come to our assistance. We courageously took down our sail, and Parsons, the oarsman, braced himself for work. We thought it would be as well to help ourselves a little, as to rely exclusively upon outside aid—that is, those of us who were not rowing thought so.

While thinking so, Wendell entertained his mother with light philosophy and persiflage, pausing occasionally to give a little sage advice to the oarsman. It is a delightful and comparatively easy task, to counsel another as to how a thing should be done. The Captain found vent for his genius in strict attention to the rudder. Our lady passenger consented, for the time being, to allow him the direction of affairs—a rare case of self-denial. What privileges Mrs. Columbus allowed her lord with respect to the rudder, we shall probably never know.

We desire to make grateful mention of the inflowing tide. It was more accommodating than the breeze, and seemed to have more vitality. As gratitude is a more distinguished virtue than disgust, it is as well to remember the favors we enjoyed, as to spend the rest of our days grumbling because they were not greater. And the tide bore us up grandly, and with a little help from the oars, rapidly, out of sight of home, up by that sweet little town named after the river, up to Rock's Bridge. There we exchanged our passenger, our better fourth, for certain articles of baggage conveyed in a carriage by friends, who had followed us on the shore to give a send-off so gracious and charming as to linger in memory with the brightest things of the morning. We took a parting look at Mary Ann, the versatile and nimble pacer, that can travel four different gaits in as many minutes, at either five or ten miles an hour, though, to her credit be it said, she prefers the five; and waving adieu to the ladies, with spirits buoyant as the Summer air, we again pushed out into the strong current. Wendell soon became impatient to row. Paddling in the water has a strange fascination for certain temperaments. And rowing with the tide seems easy when another has the oars. When affairs go prosperously, the temptation is very strong to put in an additional oar. His wish was accordingly gratified, when, with two pairs of oars, we rowed rapidly and joyously along the green shores of West Newbury, by the pines of Groveland, under the iron bridge that binds it to the Haverhill shore; and gained the port of Haverhill at two o'clock.

The view that greeted our eyes while approaching the city, like that of Salisbury Point while receding from it, was one to fasten itself in the memory.

Haverhill, with its fine public buildings, and terraces, reposing on the north bank of the river, and Bradford, with its neat, white spire, and its seminary, on the south bank, smiling in the sun at each other, and linked together by long strong bridges, formed a picture beautiful enough to inspire a painter, poet, or even three sailors. It proved so inspiring to us that we found no occasion to stop at any of the saloons for anything more exhilarating.

For the statistics of the population and business of Haverhill, and sister cities above, the reader is referred to the next gazetteer that may be published. A history like this ought not to be too heavily burdened with information. It would sadly mar its usefulness. While enjoying a sail, or following the thread of a narrative, no one wishes to clog his faculties by an accumulation of statistics. If any one really desires an exercise in figures, let him go over the multiplication table backwards.

It is to be borne in mind that history is not so much a vehicle of information as of the whims and conjectures, the preconceived opinions and moral reflections of the writer. There is another reason for refusing to mar the reader's pleasure by reference to gazetteers already published. It would look like an advertising dodge, and lead to the suspicion that the writer was actuated by mercenary motives. The historian cannot guard too jealously against this. Then again, our gazetteers have such a facile way of growing antiquated! Besides being inaccurate to begin with, they grow more and more inaccurate with the fleeting years,—thus affording a sad example of the total depravity of statistics. No, no, we could not think of referring the admirers of a growing city to any gazetteer already published. It is not only easier, but safer, to permit the reader to guess at its probable size and importance. Some historians, writing solely in the interests of truth, volunteer the guess-work themselves. There is so much of real pleasure in the work of guessing they can hardly afford to leave it to the reader.

Apparently it is easy to forget, and yet it is a fact that guess-work is not history.

We felicitate ourselves upon the next statement as an example of authentic history. At five minutes past two, while rowing under Haverhill bridge, we detected such a decided whiff of air, that we immediately put up sail and rested in our seats. The tide bore us on. The breeze seemed at first only half-hearted in its helpfulness. Apparently, it had not quite made up its mind which way to blow. There were boats waiting to go down river; and the breeze seemed half-inclined to help them at our expense. While awaiting the ultimate decision, and floating lazily with the tide, we glanced occasionally at the seminary on the hill, and wondered when the guardians of our higher institutions of learning would become sufficiently considerate to open their doors to both sexes on equal terms.

Since it is thought wise for our daughters to learn their a-b-c, it is certain that they will be educated; and if they cannot go to Harvard, or Yale, or Amherst, they must go to Bradford, Wellesley, South Hadley, or Vassar College.

But the age of monasteries and nunneries is passing away. Oberlin and Ann Arbor have been rejoicing in the dawn of a better age; and our young University at the Hub hails with open doors the new era. There is no sufficient reason, founded either in philosophy or experience, why brother and sister, who have eaten at the same table in childhood, and received correction at the same mother's knee; who have recited in the same classes in our Grammar and High schools, should be parted when they come to study that logic which forbids their separation. They may not wish all through the course to pursue exactly the same studies; but they may well be permitted to find in the same college the discipline and culture considered most desirable. But we need not fret while the age is reaching this conclusion. The night does not give way to the day suddenly. And fretting often serves to lengthen the night.

> *"This fine old world of ours is but a child,*
> *Yet in the go-cart. Patience; give it time*
> *To learn its limbs; there is a hand that guides."*

As the boys were not quite ready for college they did not apply for admission. It is hardly worth while to grumble at a closed door unless you wish to pass in. So with all cheerfulness we contemplated the closed door, and sailed on. And we did sail. The breeze taking example from the helpful tide, bore us gloriously on. And so much in earnest did it become, that after the tide turned it swept us on even against a strong current, and the noisy rapids. As blissful in our ignorance of the river before us as it is often permitted mortals to be, the pleasure of surprise was added to our experience, when the roar of waters before us greeted our ears, and the vision of several coal barges, fast on the the rocks, gave us the hint that navigation is sometimes difficult.

The breeze died away. The tide had turned. The strong current tugged at our craft, not at all uncertain of its power. But then, what are difficulties for but to quicken man's wits and whet his perseverance? The captain, that was myself, suggested that towing might be easier than rowing; and soon the line was made fast to the side of the boat, and the boys taking the other end trod the shore. By steady pulling on their part, by deft use of the captain's oar, occasionally pushing off from the rocks, we ascended the rapids known as Mitchell's Falls; and in half an hour we left them roaring and raging behind us. Flushed with the joy of victory, and with several hurrahs, we pitched our tent for the night on a handsome bluff at our left, up above the island, in a green pasture, near some oaks, birches, and walnuts, and by the side of very quiet waters. We had rowed and sailed about twenty miles, and were ready for supper and bed as soon as we could get the one, and make the other. The boys unpacked the boat with alacrity, and made their appearance at the evening meal with commendable promptness. We cut some birch boughs on which to spread the blankets, and composed ourselves to dream of the dear ones that were dreaming of us.

Slept capitally, with an occasional waking, to hear the sighing of the winds in the walnuts, and to hear Wendell and Parsons express their wonder at the hardness and size of the birch boughs beneath. But the night brought us sweet rest, a fitting preparation for an eventful day. But before entering upon that, the reader would perhaps also like a little rest. And it may as well be understood that the reader is at liberty to pause for refreshment at any time whenever the historian or himself becomes too dry.

Chapter IV. A Thunder-storm.

The sun rose the next morning with sufficient promptness. It did not seem essential for us to rise in time to greet him. Theoretically, the idea of being up with the early birds is a good one. There is a certain element of poetry in it very charming. And really it is a delightful thing to dream about. Nature's sweet restorer was lingering near our pillow. Yet we can hardly think it was on account of any attractiveness in the pillow. A bundle of rope is not soft as downy pillows are. The thundering of the trains within a half-mile of our encampment was not encouraging to sleep; and soon the thundering of the clouds gave the voice of Old Prob. respecting the next fortnight. We took it as a signal for rising. When it began to rain we concluded not to build a camp-fire. Considering that we had no suitable wood, it was a wise conclusion. Were we not fortunate in having a camp-stove? The shower was soon over, and it threatened so decidedly to clear off, that we quickly loaded our ship and rowed leisurely for Lawrence. We passed another coal barge secure upon the rocks, waiting either a rise in the river or a rise in coal. We soon passed the steeples of North Andover on our left, and rested for a little in a birch grove just opposite the mouth of the Shawsheen, and a little below the outlet of the Lawrence canal. During the interval of rest we discussed the project of rowing up the Shawsheen, and climbing Andover Hill to see if there was a spark of genuine orthodoxy left to illumine that old theological watch-tower which has such a wonderful *faculty* of renewing her youth. Cherishing a grateful remembrance of the cheerful and wholesome instruction given there, we could not help breathing an invocation to Heaven that the Star of Bethlehem might ever be the pole-star of her theology. Remembering, however, that those were vacation days, we concluded that it would be as well to leave the whole matter to the care of Heaven as to undertake ourselves to regulate it. In the theological world a little confidence is better, perhaps, than a good deal of dictation. We are saved by faith, not by fault-finding.

We were within sound of the work-shops of a city that contains about as much industry to the square mile as any in New England, but which only a third of a century ago was almost a wilderness. At noon we lifted our dory up the bank, a carry of a dozen rods, and embarked on the canal to run the gauntlet of a score of bridges.

Our ride up to the upper lock was like a triumphal march, cheered by hundreds if not thousands of the sons and daughters of industry, crossing the bridges, and stopping to wave their caps and handkerchiefs to the "sailors," and speak a word perchance of applause or friendly banter.

Before the hour of their rest was over we had rowed up the long canal and been locked through into the river above the dam—a magnificent structure, affording a little Niagara of twenty feet.

While taking our dinner in the edge of a pine forest just above the city, we were startled by the appearance of the first bear which we had thus far encountered. It was a huge black one, that had climbed a dead tree, and was making threatening gestures. Another look revealed the fact that there were two of them; and we had not caught in the city the trick of seeing double, either. The second was standing erect, and showing his glittering teeth. We had net expected to find bears so early in our trip, nor so near the borders of civilization. And the pleasure of surprise was even greater than our fear of danger. They were not quite near enough to be effective as quickeners of the conscience. But there they were; and neither showed any inclination to run. Our weapons were in the boat, and the gun was unloaded. Not having the experience of the ancient shepherd lad, that slew a lion and a bear, as the record runs, Wendell was loath to grapple with them empty-handed. He was apparently not hungry for bear's meat. Possibly they were hungrier than he. Parsons was already out of sight, behind a tree. He had started in search of a grazing farm, to inquire for milk. And it is quite doubtful whether Wendell could have handled the bears alone. Besides, he was having about all he could do to save himself and dinner from a crow that had determined to have a meal at his expense. He concluded in the circumstances not to go for the bears. The captain was too busy to interfere; naturally of a peaceable disposition, he thought it unbecoming in a naval commander to engage in war upon land. Then again, the bears had felt restrained from making any attack. And the idea of an offensive war is not in harmony with the traditions of a Christian people.

We saw also in the wood, a fox and some wild geese, but concluded not to load our gun. That was not our hunting ground. "Discretion is the better part of valor;" it was then. We had not planned to engage in the hunt so early in our voyage, and were too conservative to think of changing our plans.

After dinner a favoring breeze filled the sail, and bore us easily on from four to five miles in a southwesterly course, when threatened with a thunder-shower, we landed in a pine forest in Tewksbury—a splendid camping ground. Before we could pitch our tent, or get the baggage ashore, a tempest of thunder and lightning swept down upon us. We covered some articles with rubber blankets, and took others with us to the shelter of the dense pines, and from a good look-out watched the progress of the storm. The war of the elements was both sublime and terrific—terrific to any of a timid temperament; but it was grandly inspiring, calling forth our faith in Him who wields the artillery of heaven. A dark and ominous cloud, apparently moving west from Methuen, sent bolts of lightning thick and fast straight to the earth; it was met by another that seemed to move in the opposite direction, or down from Dracut. The contest was furious; sharp, crackling thunder spoke the anger of the elements, and the lightning seemed incessant.

Meanwhile the rain poured in torrents; and distant thunder rolling and roaring, gave evidence of the storm raging to the south and west of us. For a time it seemed uncertain which of the contending clouds would gain the victory, or which way the storm would pass. Then it appeared to be moving eastward, and to rage most furiously over Lawrence. Again it appeared to return, move upward, and spend its fury in the vicinity of Lowell.

It probably had a far wider range. We attempt only a description of what appeared to us.

At length light broke in in the direction of the northeast, and the rain poured less furiously. At six o'clock the sun was shining, and the storm was over. He was right welcome—and we gave him cordial greeting.

How fared it with the sailors in the wood, do you ask?

Two of us with the basket of provisions had the shelter of the umbrella; and Parsons, with the ingenuity of an Edison, made a shelter-tent for himself with an old waterproof cloak, his mother's last blessing, by fastening three corners of it to three pines that stood near together and holding up the middle of it with an oar.

His tent was in appearance more ludicrous than graceful; but it was useful. And in the matter of shelter-tents utility should have precedence over beauty—especially during the rainy season.

His kept him dry. None of us were wet. And the facts of history will warrant the further statement that during the series of thunder-storms that followed that Friday none of us received a wetting before the return home.

When the sun came out we chose a place for encampment, looking about a little to see if any of us were struck with lightning. So nimble and numerous had been the electric fairies, that we could hardly believe our grove unvisited. No trace of harm appeared. We took our ship through an inlet round to a delightful harbor, quite hidden from the river. A grassy knoll, a little removed from the trees, but well concealed, offered hospitality to our tent.

We kindled our campfire, not without difficulty. The shower had not inspired the wood with any enthusiasm. But the pines stood ready to sacrifice their pitch on our altar. So pitch and perseverance gained the victory. A substantial supper of oatmeal mush and milk satisfied our hunger. Two sons of Nimrod, who had protected themselves by fastening up their sail to two trees, offered to show the way to a Summer apple tree in an adjoining orchard. As the tree belonged neither to them nor us, we declined the offer, and had no reason to regret the decision, after learning that the apples were hard. Virtue is its own reward, when it saves one from the colic.

An abundance of pine leaves afforded material for comfortable beds. Rubber blankets kept out the dampness, or rather kept it in; and the the rheumatism that was lurking beneath was disappointed of its prey. Soon after eight, we disposed ourselves for the night, and lulled to sleep by the murmuring pines, we rested as sweetly and peacefully under the care of Heaven's angels, as though earth had never known a storm.

Chapter V. The Broken Oar.

The hill at the east of our camp, and the dense pines prevented the day from breaking too early upon our slumbers. So after a long sleep we awoke refreshed, ready for fresh adventures.

O the wonder of sleep, that sweet oblivion that makes man young, and the world beautiful once more! With what eager hope one hails a new day, when the beautiful Morn holds out her hands of promise and of blessing! Old as time, the world rests upon the shoulders of hoary Atlas, and yet smiles with the grace of immortal youth, when she turns her brow to the sun for her morning kiss.

A slight fog on the river gave token of a fair day. We boiled our pudding over the campfire, and with milk, sandwiches, and turnovers, made the morning meal.

While Parsons was gone for the milk, Wendell took his first lessons in loading and shooting the gun.

There was no difficulty in loading. The trial of fortitude and patience came in with the shooting. It proved a trial of perseverance also. Wendell, pointing the terrible weapon at an innocent tree, pulled the trigger. Snap!—but no bang! Well, it was not the first time a youth had been disappointed in a gun. Sometimes the disappointment precedes, and sometimes it follows the discharge.

"Perhaps the fault is in the cap; try another," suggested the captain.

"I did," responded the marksman.

"No go?"

"No."

"Try again, better luck next time!"

"Bang!" spoke the gun; and without any thought of advising the boy to turn idiot in the style of combing his hair; though it made every hair stand on end.

"There is some go in the gun, after all; or else in the powder. What have you hit?"

"Oh! hit pretty much all round."

"Kick any?"

"Only a little. She hasn't learned how."

"Load her up once more. You can teach her by putting in a little more powder."

"I'm not playing schoolmaster now."

"Nor the coward, I hope?"

"The what?"

"There! d'ye see that rabbit? Load up quick; he'll be gone."

Wendell loads again, and creeps along by the underbrush, under the brow of the hill, till he imagines he has found the right place.

"Snap," again said the gun quickly, as though she didn't care a snap for the rabbit.

"Once more I" shouted the captain.

"Snap, bang!" before the words were fairly out of his mouth.

We didn't have fried rabbit for breakfast; but we had number one appetites. And appetites without rabbits are even better than rabbits without appetites, particularly when you have some other choice delicacy. We had a good breakfast. And as the rabbits had also the opportunity of enjoying their breakfast, perhaps the amount of happiness was quite as great as though they had furnished the meal. The ham sandwiches removed all sense of disappointment from the stomach of the marksman. The pudding disappeared somehow, not very mysteriously; and the turnover pies proved a fine dessert. Wendell forgave the old musket her little eccentricities; and with all cheerfulness washed the dishes and loaded the boat, while with equal cheerfulness Parsons made the attempt to hook a few fish from our trout brook. He found them. He admired their appearance and size, but not their behavior. He was compelled, however, to admire their sagacity. All fish are not sagacious. Like many a silly youth who bites at a bare hook, they sometimes give indication of a sad lack of discretion. But these were not indiscreet. They were wise enough and patient enough to wait for a more expert fisherman. Their admirer has been more successful since, more than once, in obtaining fish at the markets.

At half-past eight we took in anchor and rowed leisurely for Lowell. The fog was lifted from the river, leaving a surface smooth as a polished mirror. We could see not only the beautiful shores, but their reflection in the water, sweet banks, delightful groves, and precipitous bluffs, as beautiful below as above, showing that nature has a double charm for her lovers. A few miles brought us to stronger currents, where the water rippled and gurgled with its swifter motion.

Our oarsmen were put upon their muscle. Stronger still the current grew; and we could hear the roaring of the rapids above. A dense smoke was ascending from behind the high banks on the north. This and the fine residences on the bluff below Lowell indicated that we had almost reached the city. But the river showed no signs of becoming propitious; with a more angry roar it greeted our coming.

It became a practical study for us, how we were to ascend the rapids. The boys had rowed manfully up to their very feet, when the whitecaps, and the boiling, tumbling flood seemed to say, "Thus far shalt thou go, and no farther." There appeared no chance for a carry. But we found our opportunity for further progress behind a little island on the north side. Rowing up to the upper end, we found the water shoal; and Wendell prepared to ford it a little way.

Rolling up their pants, the boys took the boat between them, and guided her among the rocks up past the first difficult point. Then with the tow-line they endeavored to pull her by the next difficult place, where the current was too swift and deep for fording. Walking along the rocky edge, they tugged away bravely, while with oar in hand we sought to keep her off the rocks and headed in the right direction. It was hard to prevent capsizing. In the place of greatest peril, snap went the tow-line, and we were seemingly at the mercy of the angry flood. Tossed on the breakers like a chip, our bark was the play of the exulting victor. Swiftly the wild current was bearing us down, and the distance between us and the Atlantic Ocean was growing rapidly less. But a few vigorous strokes of the oar, a little extra pull, brought us to shore, and we were ready to try again. Working up once more to the same difficult point, we tried next time with the anchor-line, together with our towline, to pull her through, this time successfully. So we worked our way up to a point where by reason of precipitous rocks, towing was impossible. The current was too swift for fording. In attempting it, Parsons slipped, sat down in the water, and escaped drowning by clinging to the edge of the boat. He did not wait to dry his pantaloons at that time. By dint of continuous effort we gained another point; but only to find more terrible rapids before us, and a more difficult shore. To cross the river seemed our only resource. It was to all appearance a perilous undertaking. Could we keep our boat headed up stream, and pull with sufficient steadiness to avoid upsetting, or drifting into the whirling eddies below us? We could try; and we did it. In spite of the pull which the current gave us, we gained the south shore. Here was opportunity to repeat the toil that had brought us up so far. There was still no chance for a carry; and we had to make our way slowly round the rocks. In rowing around one where there was no chance for towing, snap went an oar, one of our best pair, and we should have come to grief, had not Parsons, quick as a flash, grasped another, and pulled us manfully through. As it was, grief came to us, for no such oar as the broken one could be obtained in Lowell. And we could not wait to have one made. A young Hibernian, coming to our assistance for his own amusement, thought he could get more fun out of it by "bossing the job;" and so began to give orders. The enjoyment of the original captain was so great in his officiousness that he turned the whole matter of command over to the stranger and appointed himself first mate. To work our way up to the upper rapids was a comparatively easy matter. There, at the foot of Stackpole Street, we transferred our vessel from the river to a furniture wagon, having for assistants two of the sons, or great-grandsons of Ethiopia, who preferred to help us up the bank, rather than continue their own work. As that was beating carpets, we did not feel like blaming them too severely. We did not blame them half so much as we do the man who invented an institution that requires beating so often.

In an hour we had crossed the city to the river above the dam. Not wishing to waste our time by any idle curiosity while passing through the city, we meditated upon the lessons our experience had taught us; first, to adjust your efforts to the strength of the material with which you have to deal; don't exert yourself foolishly; secondly, not to risk too much upon one oar or a single line.

The old woman had learned the same lesson when she said she would not trust all her eggs in one basket.

We had received also a fresh illustration of the fact that though nature is sometimes indulgent toward her children, she does not always favor them with cheap success. Sometimes she gives them a kiss, and sometimes a cuff; and often she leaves them to learn that the joy of victory is gained only by strenuous battle. But we had the victory; and our boat was above the Falls.

Having replenished our stores at Lowell, we rowed on, without stopping to visit the habitations of man or take note of the mills.

Had we not come from a mills village?—and was it not the river we had started to explore? What was Lowell to us, more than London, or New York, or Boston? We had visited the city before, and knew of its sweet and generous hospitality, and wonderful enterprises. Gratefully remembering the one, and greatly admiring the other, we waved adieu without a pang, and pulled for other shores. Up, past the village of North Chelmsford, past the Wickesauke Island, and great rafts of logs, turning with the river to the west, where it broadens to a bay, we rowed and sailed by turns, full of delight with the ever varying scene, into the sweet twilight, where we pitched our tent for the night some five or six miles above Lowell, in the most restful little nook that ever weary pilgrims were fortunate enough to find after dark. Under a buttonwood tree, near a large white birch, on the north bank, we slept all the more profoundly for our strenuous toiling. Neither the rippling river nor the winds of heaven disturbed our slumbers.

Chapter VI. our First Sunday.

It was the first Sunday in August. We were in camp on the east side of the river, a little above Lowell. We had found the place after dark, and could not tell the name of the town. But it does not make so much difference in what town you spend the Sabbath, as in what manner. The spot was one of the most attractive and bewitching out of doors; and the morning was so radiant that we did not care for a place within doors. The commandment does not specify whether you shall keep the Sabbath day holy under a roof of slate, pine shingles, cloth, or blue sky. It allows great liberty. But its spirit would secure a rest-day for toil-worn humanity. Rest does not mean revelry.

We had explored Wickesauke Island for a place to camp over the Sabbath, but found that since the red man had omitted to hold his powows there, the white Indians from Lowell had consecrated the Island to a worse carousal. Sabbath desecration and drinking were not the only faults of its uncivilized visitors. We not only did not wish to intrude upon such company, but we preferred for ourselves a place of rest to one of revelry; and notwithstanding the offer of the enterprising proprietor, to let us set up our tent over Sunday, for the modest sum of one dollar, we chose to continue our explorations and pull for another shore. Nature could hardly have rewarded us with a more delightful retreat than the grassy bluff where our tent was pitched. We did not know how beautiful it was till the Sabbath sun revealed it. It was in the upper extremity of an orchard that had been mown, where fine elms, oaks, and small birches afforded shade and a secluded retreat, and where the green terraces of still higher banks shut off all view from the street. Next us was a wooded ravine through which a trout brook gurgled, and where huckleberries grew, and were sweetly ripening that Sunday. It was indeed a resting-place. But rest does not imply utter cessation from all activity.

The most delightful Sunday rest may call into active exercise the higher faculties of our nature. It is not inconsistent with regular church attendance. And it is a question whether there is any better way for a well man to spend a part of Sunday, if the walk is not over five miles, than to attend some place of worship. To join in the service with other devout souls, is helpful to "the divinity within."

Inquiring for a church at the nearest farmhouse, where we had gone for milk, we were directed to the one they called Orthodox, as the others were having a vacation.

We found a congregation of about seventy-five, in a pretty little meeting-house, almost new, and a young minister with a pleasant face and voice, quite in keeping with the pleasant morning. The opening service was admirably adapted to cheer and refresh the weary, and awaken emotions of reverence, and gratitude. The sermon was a plain one, easy of comprehension, on the duty of self-denial. It was suggestive, rather than exhaustive, and yet it was long enough to exhaust the interest of the congregation. Ten minutes' abbreviation would have rendered it doubly effective.

The flourish of announcements in the introduction was a little out of proportion to its contents. It is perhaps as well to say what one has to say without wasting the time in prophesying what is going to be said. The old style of sermonizing used to be to foretell in the introduction what the speaker intended to say in the body of the discourse, then say it over again with amplifications, and in conclusion tell what had been said in the discussion. The plan had its advantages, for those accustomed to sleep through two-thirds of sermon time. But it is not the preacher's first duty to encourage sleep.

In this more busy age, it suffices to say a good thing once, if you only say it well. But the discourse that day was not modeled upon either the old plan, or any more recent method of sermonizing; it was not open to the objection of being too strictly conformed to any plan; but possessed somewhat of the interest which attaches to an unpremeditated ramble in the woods. It was a problem with preacher and hearer alike as to where he would come out. It was a poor enough sermon in some particulars, and yet it was worth going to hear. It was a great deal better worth going to hear than many of the sermons preached in some city pulpits. For singular as it may seem, some of our city ministers think they have as good a right to preach poor sermons as any of our country parsons. And it would seem to some of their hearers that they had preached so many of them, that their brethren in the country might well be excused from adding to the number.

We cherish grateful recollections of the sermon for two things; that it was so free from the cant of philosophy, which mars so many modern discourses; and that it made no attempt to resurrect the ghosts of dead doctrines which in generations gone by have been mistaken as orthodox.

And we think great allowance should be made for a young preacher, who is required to write two sermons a week, besides undergoing all the wear and tear of pastoral labors. The wonder is that a man can find anything to say after the first few weeks; or get time to learn anything new.

It mattered little to us, that the preacher had not learned what to do with his hands, nor how to construct his discourses, nor what to put into them; our solicitude was aroused most of all for the congregation that had not learned to practise the self-denial taught in the sermon,, and forego the pleasure of listening to so many weak discourses, that would have been stronger if reduced in number and dimensions.

Congregations as well as ministers have much to learn with regard to the best way of administering the trusts committed to them.

It is a great satisfaction to most of us that our neighbors generally have yet much to learn. And how fortunate that we are generally so competent to give them wise counsel!

It is a practical question for all our churches, how to hold our men and boys.

A noticeable feature of the congregation, was the scarcity of men, and almost entire absence of boys.

While on our way to church we could not restrain our pity for two disconsolate looking youth, who were holding their fishing tackle by the bank of the stream, laboring under the delusion that New England fish would bite on Sunday. We pitied them that they should prefer angling when the prospect was so poor, to attending church; but after the service, our pity was divided between them and the congregation that could not provide a service more attractive for New England youth than any form of Sabbath desecration.

Returning, we rested in our grove, and thought upon the presumptuous youth, who was so indiscreet as to drop a line on Sunday to fish that have no care for such communications even on the other days of the week.

Then occurred that declaration of the Master, pronounced on the shores of Galilee—" I will make you fishers of men." And the question kept recurring, when he laid the emphasis upon men, did he mean that his preachers should secure the allegiance only of their mothers and sisters? The good Father says—" All souls are mine." Are not the boys and young men souls as truly as their mothers and sisters? The plain answer is affirmative. Nor can it be shown that the young men think less of their souls, or less of serious and manly things, than do their sisters. The simple fact is, they require a manly, not an effeminate exposition of Christianity. Such a proclamation of it will receive their attention. When they are convinced that Christianity is the science of true manhood, and genuine womanhood, they will accompany their wives and sisters to church. The preacher or church that would secure the attention and respect of the men must give them something to attend to. That is their reasonable service.

The little church on the banks of the Merrimac, where it was our good fortune to attend worship is not our target. It is not more open to criticism than many of its sister churches.

But if the churches of the Merrimac Valley wish to consult the highest interests of our Redeemer's kingdom, they should endeavor so to administer, proclaim, and illustrate their Christianity as to gain the attention, the respect, and the allegiance of the most thoughtful minds. They are to become "fishers of men."

The river flowed on without a murmur, undisturbed by the muttering thunder. And ages hence, fed by the rains of heaven, it will continue to flow. Other generations will tread these shores, and shade themselves under the descendants of these oaks, and will lift their hearts in worship and their voices in praise to Him, who is the same yesterday, and today, and forever.

We need not greatly vex ourselves because of any imperfections that we note in our neighbors. Though this is not to be construed as favoring any indulgence of our own imperfections. Yet the good Father is wonderfully patient. If He bears with our follies, shall not we bear with them, until we can correct them?

Really, there is no better time to begin this good work than Sunday. There is no heterodoxy in trying to mend our lives on any day. Though the grand Cardinal of Mendoza thought the plan of Columbus for discovering America savored strongly of heterodoxy, there is none in any sincere plan for sailing to that undiscovered country, whose citizens make no mistakes, since they have at command the resources of infinite Wisdom and infinite Love.

Chapter VII. Onward and Upward.

Refreshed by a Sabbath's rest, not having wearied ourselves with too much grumbling nor too many services, we were ready Monday morning for a new start, and fresh adventures.

The sky was clear, the breeze favorable; we put up sail, and bade good-bye to the birds singing in our grove, with hearts as light as theirs. We passed the old town of Tyngsborough at nine o'clock, saw the morning train from Boston loaded with passengers for the mountains, and we could not help pitying them, as they were snatched along and whirled away from that delightful scenery, of which they could get only glimpses, while we on our sail could leisurely feast to the fill, and delight our eyes with the sweet pictures. Winding our way up the crooked stream, we came at every turn to some new beauty, yielding a fresh delight and an added stimulus.

Sweet fields of grain or meadow grass, fresh pastures where flocks and herds were grazing, groves of pine, oak, or birch, musical with birds, higher and bolder banks, and forests stretching far back from the river, gave variety and at times the charm of wildness to the scenery.

We missed the pleasant farm-houses and large barns which had continually reminded us that we were in a civilized country.

Gradually the current grew stronger, and occasionally gurgled and boiled as though angry with the rocks strewn so thickly in the river bed. No wonder the uneasy waters were eager to leave a bed so rough!

But the breeze was stronger than the current, and bore us onward with an ease and inspiration to be remembered gratefully. At a little after twelve we reached the old wooden bridge that crosses the Merrimac from Nashua to Hudson, and landed on the west bank, the Nashua side, just above the bridge, where we found a cool, grassy hollow, sweet enough for a camping-ground, shaded by three elms, one ash, one cotton-wood, and a yellow pine, under which we took our noonday meal. It is not recorded that Washington ever rallied his troops under either of the elms of that little grove; but their shade was just as agreeable as though they had enjoyed intimate acquaintance with the General. Had he reviewed his army there a dozen times, or had the ancestors of Sitting Bull built there their camp-fires, the fact would hardly have added to the delicate flavor of the apples which we had for dessert. They were beautiful Red Astrachans, whose rich and sprightly acid reminds one of the wit of those sparkling conversationalists that delight to startle more humdrum people with their brilliant paradoxes. If this were a chapter of advice we should commend every reader who would like an early apple tree to plant a Red Astrachan the very next season in commemoration of the satisfaction we took in those lively beauties.

Nashua, to all appearances, was a little hamlet but little removed from the bank of the river; but is really a city of twelve or fourteen thousand, situated on the Nashua River, a mile above its mouth, and from which it derives an abundance of waterpower for its many shops.

It is memorable to us, however, chiefly as the home of Louis Heald, a boy of ten, perhaps, and bright and good enough to be the hero of a Sunday-school book.

When we packed our luncheon basket, we left a knife on the ground under the elms. And when, on our return trip ten days afterward, we were taking dinner on the same spot, it was our pleasant surprise to see the honest lad coming again to greet us, and bringing the knife, apparently more glad to return it than we were to recover it. We were far more delighted to see the boy again than to see the knife; for we remembered his gentlemanly deportment to us as strangers, his readiness in answering our inquiries, and helpfulness in procuring the apples. The charm of the first acquaintance was renewed, and we were glad to meet once more a lad whose conduct reflected so much honor upon both his parents and the city of Nashua. When his future biographer shall give the record of his life, it will not be strange if he shall have occasion to speak of his honest administration as mayor of the city, or Governor of his native state. But let him not forget to mention his cheerful and manly deportment in the matter of the stranger's knife. Happy the parents, and happy the city, that can point to such children and say, "These are my jewels." Taking him for the type of the Merrimac Valley boy, who says that the rising generation is not going to be honest? It may be early in the day to nominate the Governor of New Hampshire for 1910, but if we were a nominating convention it would give us great pleasure to mention the name of Louis Heald, of Nashua, a manly boy, who will certainly be too modest to think of nominating himself.

It affords us great satisfaction here to mention, by way of supplement to the history of the first voyage of Columbus, that he discovered no such boy in all his long journey.

Starting after dinner, with a fresh southerly breeze, we sailed quickly by the mouth of the Nashua, whose industrious waters came tumbling into the Merrimac, and by some strange-looking river craft, made of barrel hoops and painted cloth, and up five or six miles between precipitous banks, till, long before night, we reached a delightful camping-ground somewhere in Merrimac, N. H. We pitched tent and swung the hammock in a pine and birch grove, on a high bluff that by its many attractions abundantly rewarded some rather difficult climbing. Grassy intervals, alternating with small pines, clumps of bushes, and open spaces, formed a place for encampment fine enough for a park. Farther down river we had been surprised to find so many beautiful camping-grounds occupied by permanent residences. Here, and farther up river, we were equally surprised to find so many charming nooks and corners unoccupied. At nightfall Wendell and Parsons went in swimming, and frollicked like old sturgeon in their native element. Their joyous shouts awoke the echoes on the other shore, and called forth many boisterous responses from others swimming in the distance.

Swinging in our hammock, we fell asleep and made it our bed for the night. The boys slept in the tent. The only incident of the night was a scare, which resulted from the going out of the lantern. It appeared that our camping-ground was a calf-pasture; and attracted by the light within the tent the calves had gathered near, and were mentally ruminating upon the character of their strange guests. They were reaching a somewhat unfavorable conclusion, as Wendell tried at various times to drive them away, when the lantern suddenly went out. Filled with wonder and alarm they started as if shot, and ran bellowing as though all the fiends of darkness were after them. It did not seem imperative that we should follow. We had not mistaken them for bears or deer. We were not hungry for veal.

The last we knew of those calves they were running for dear life, with no perils to pursue them. How like some men of timid temperament, who run the swiftest before imaginary dangers! But it is not necessary to be very timid in order to make a large-sized mistake. In fact, the making of mistakes is a kind of manufacture in which persons of all temperaments, and every variety of talents, can engage. It does not require the intellect of a Bacon, nor the genius of a Milton. It is a grievous mistake to make a fool of one's self; but a calf can do that.

Tuesday morning the boys cooked their breakfast of pudding and eggs while the birds sang their matins and the steam-whistles gave their signals for work. It was our call to breakfast; and surely never breakfast tasted better. A row of half a mile brought us not very quickly—for it was like rowing up hill—to Coos Falls,where there is the wreck of an old canal, built to aid navigation. It offered us no assistance. We were compelled to row up to the foot of the falls, and tow our ship up its steep places without the help of the locks. This we did without loss, although a stranger cheerfully informed us that a party just a little before us had their boat upset, and lost their tent and shoes. Mingling our sorrows for their loss with rejoicing over our better fortune, we put up sail and before a brisk wind sped northward as straight as the crooked river would carry us. The music of merry voices drew our attention to some noble elms on the bank, under which sat a bevy of bright Boston girls engaged with books and fancy work. Parsons went ashore to inquire for a farm-house where he could fill his pail with water; and they insisted on guiding him to the well, and as gracefully and cheerfully as Rebekah of old they gave him drink.

The simplicity of nature and the refinement of culture blended so beautifully in their deportment, we could not but think that those daughters of the Graces esteemed it a favor to be permitted to grant a favor.

A little further up river, where the Souhegan joins the Merrimac, as we looked under the bridge, we caught a glimpse of a landscape like a picture set in a frame, charming enough to take an artist's eye, and engage his pencil.

We stopped for dinner on Naticook Island, near Reed's Ferry, and in the shade of its grand old elms, from tables put up for some picnic, we ate our bread and milk, crackers and cheese, and apples for dessert. The island had recently been called by the old Indian name, Minnewahwah. It was also known as Reed's Island. Having three names, the river had kindly consented to cut it into three distinct portions; but as the river was low, the three were one again. Above the island the current was very strong, and it took an hour or more to row up half or three-quarters of a mile to the foot of another fall. As we made our way through the roaring rapids the thunder began also to roar from ominous-looking clouds, which sent us into camp. Sheltered by the tent, unmindful of the storm. Parsons took the paper and gleaned it for information, and Wendell a book, soon forgetting that there was any outside world, or any such thing as time. O the power of the press to drive away ennui, and lead its victims or its patrons to the realms of forgetfulness! What would not Horace have given for a Boston daily to relieve the tedium of his journey to Brundusium! What would not Noah have offered for a copy of the "Wide Awake," during that prolonged rainy season, which caused such disaster to all the railroads that no trains were run for more than three thousand years!

Chapter VIII. Rowing up-Stairs.

Night set in with a succession of thunder showers. One after another came roaring down the valley, and pouring down its contributions to the river. Our slumbers were somewhat disturbed by this prolonged serenade. And once we awoke to find a pool of water just under our pillow. A newspaper laid carelessly against the canvass had conveyed the drip carefully to the said pool. It thus proved its capacity to be a vehicle of moist as well as of dry facts. To remove the intruding flood was a far less serious matter than drowning. It required less time. To remove the paper, less yet. Then lighting our stove to take the chill from the air, we slept sweetly, with out further disturbance, until the birds sang their welcome to the new day.

It was a very promising morning. It promised to be fair. It promised to be hot. It promised us a plenty of hard work. Two-thirds of these promises were faithfully kept. While the potatoes and oatmeal were cooking, one of the boys visited a hospitable farm-house and procured supplies of milk and bread, and the other bailed the boat, and prepared for an early start. After breakfast we girded ourselves for action; and found an hour's perilous work in ascending Moore's falls, whose music had mingled with the roar of thunder during the night. We made the passage of the falls through the old canal, finding but three points of special danger and difficulty. By rowing, towing, lifting and carrying, we gained the victory, and were ready for further endeavor. The falls were full of big boulders that were adorned with the wrecks of less fortunate vessels. The workmen on the railroad from the opposite bank of the river swung their hats, and shouted "hurrah," as if to celebrate our triumph. This proved the first of a succession of victories, to gain which occupied the day. After the first mile of rowing the current became provokingly strong, affording us a strong pull for a very little gain. The bed of the river began to look as though sown with rocks of all sizes and shapes. One in particular was large enough to reach nearly half-across the river. It would have made a solid foundation for a large house. We explored it, named it Rock Island, and rowed on. But our progress onward was very slow— though upward it was very fast. We rowed as it were upstairs, pretty much all day. We would climb the falls to find others roaring just ahead. The canals that had once been a help to navigation were in such dilapidated condition as to be attractive chiefly as ruins. Large stones once forming symmetrical walls, were tumbled in delightful confusion, stained with age, and grown over with vines and bushes. They contributed not a little to the romance of the scene, but very little to the ease of our journey. The old locks were but piles of rocks in our way. A little willow grove just below the railroad bridge at Goff's Falls invited us to lunch that noon. Heaven's artillery furnished the musical accompaniment. We were admonished of a coming hurricane. A strange darkness filled the northern sky. But the covered bridge offered us shelter. We hastened to reach it, rowing up through the rapids, and landing nearly under the west end.

To carry our baggage and equipments to the pier, and load it with heavy stones; to take our little ship up the rocks and make it secure above the falls; then to dispose ourselves safely in the bridge, required less time than the storm-god took for his preliminary howl. But as soon as we were ready, he gave us to understand that his menaces were not mere bravado. Down the river he came, astride a regular tornado, growling and roaring, breathing a terrible flame, hurling bolts of fierce lightning in all directions, and pouring out a deluge of rain, to prevent a general conflagration.

We were grateful to his majesty for so timing the tempest as to give us the opportunity of gaining such adequate shelter. No tent could have stood before such a sweeping gale. For over an hour the rain poured, and the lightning played; and yet it struck nothing nearer to us than a telegraph pole at the farther end of the bridge.

After the storm had gone to confer its favors upon those further down river, we replenished our provisions at the grocery a quarter of a mile away, and rowed up a half-mile or more to Short's Falls, where we made another climb of six feet in thirty rods, without serious accident, though not without serious effort. Our day's work was nearly done. Our ambition was satisfied. Rowing round a curve in the river, we spied in the distance a wooded island. The setting sun was taking his last look at her beauty. Glad and grateful we pulled for the inviting shore, and after brief exploration, chose our place of encampment on a high, grassy bluff, easy of ascent, and pitched tent, driving in the stakes strongly, thinking to rest for a few days and take an inventory of our discoveries. We slept that night the sweet sleep that heaven vouchsafes to mortals wearied with climbing upward; on that island in mid-river, as solitary as if in mid-ocean, its only occupants, we slept as unconsciously as the first sinless pair in their unstained Eden.

Chapter ix. Passaconaway Island.

One week from the time we started from home, we awoke to behold our New-found-land, and find it one of the loveliest and yet wildest of all the islands of the Merrimac. It was not quite so large as the other Newfoundland; if it had been, it would have been altogether too large for the river. Ours was just the right size, holding its place easily, without putting the river to too much trouble to get round it. As an island, wild, romantic, and beautiful, it filled our ideal for a resting-place, and satisfied our thirst for discovery. Upon further exploration the enchantment grew not less but greater. Ours was the only dwelling place upon the island, and we had abundance of room; somewhere from six to eight acres. It was nearly a quarter of a mile long, and wide enough for a fine building lot.

Here were groves of pine, some ancient and ambitious, almost piercing the sky; some young and resinous, filling the air with their delicate aroma. There were groves of hemlock fringing the most charming hiding places with their bewitching foliage. There were groves of elm and oak, and of birch and maple. There were screens of under brush for the birds and squirrels.

There were intervals of grass, soft and yielding, carpeting our yard and adjoining spaces. There were beautiful mosses, delicate enough to repay careful observation and prolonged study; and some dry and elastic, just the material for beds and pillows.

There were clumps of sumac lifting their scarlet-crowned peduncles in the air, and by their peculiar foliage, reminding one of their tropical neighbors. Here and there were clumps of flowers, bright-eyed asters, ambitious golden-rod, and the most elegant thistles, whose purple crowns were in sweet odor, and musical with the hum of bees. Other more modest flowers looked heavenward in sweet humility. A group of white birchs stood as sentinels by our camp-fire; and old trees vied with their younger neighbors in the abundance of fuel offered to replenish the dying embers. Thus the old and the young entered into the most generous rivalry as to which should do the most good. As was most fitting, the older ones won the palm, for they had improved the years in gathering substance to bestow.

How grateful we ought to be to Time for the opportunity of gathering somewhat with which to enrich our successors! There were many sermons in those old trees that gave of their abundance to replenish our fire. We became withal pretty devoted fire-worshippers, considering it was the month of August. When the sun smiled on us, we adored the sun. When the lightnings flashed, and that was not infrequently, we stood in awe before the lightning. And at sunset or before, when there were no thundershowers, we built bon-fires and paid our evening devotions. When the rain drove us into tent, as it grew fond of doing, we lighted our kerosene stove and basked in its beneficence. We were reminded again and again that we had chosen the rainy season for our excursion, and that thunder-storms were all the fashion. But would we as lief be out of the world as out of the fashion? Would we?

We were not without consolation, as we thought the friends at home were enjoying the same free exhibition of heaven's fireworks. And they were very splendid. Never was lightning more nimble than that which played all around us; nor was any more successful at dodging, for it dodged our island completely, though many a noble pine offered very flattering inducements to the electric fairies to come and settle with us. It is said that thunder-showers like to follow the course of the river. It is hardly an exaggeration to say that on one day, Friday, several dozen of them betrayed their liking for following its course. For they came one after another in a succession so close that it was impossible to tell where one left off and the next one began. Often it seemed as though the next began before its predecessor was ready to leave off.

But notwithstanding the brilliant weather, the island grew more dear to us day by day. No amount of rain seemed to dampen in the least the high spirits of our crew. And wonderfully refreshing was the content that lingered around our encampment.

Swinging in our hammock, when the weather was kind enough to permit it, we thought of our good fortune as contrasted with that of Columbus, when after almost infinite trials, he brought his mutinous crew to that little heap of coral in the Atlantic, which he named San Salvador. In all our journeying, amid all perils, when the lightning had been most fierce, when the waves had rolled the highest, not one of the crew had shown any trace of a mutinous spirit, or refused to go on with us in the discovery of our new world; but ever ready for action, and eager to advance, each had shown himself worthy to be at least the fourteenth cousin of Columbus himself. We had a splendid crew—ourselves even being the judges. Then, as to our comparative successes, we had abundant reason to felicitate ourselves. At the end of his voyage Columbus did not really know what he had found. It was only a little island inhabited by barbarians; and the neighboring islands were as full of barbarians as that. We must remember that he did not discover the whole of America; nor did he find anywhere on his way any such enterprising and thrifty cities as we had found on the banks of the Merrimac. He sailed by no Haverhills, nor Lawrences, nor Lowells, nor Nashuas, nor Manchesters; but he was almost convulsed with joy at finding a little island full of savages, and blown upon by fierce tornadoes—a little island whose only claim to distinction from that day to this has been that the brave explorer once set foot upon it.

On the other hand we knew what we had discovered,—beautiful cities shining on the Merrimac like pearls on a necklace; fine farms and elegant farm-houses, the homes of gentlemen as much more learned than Columbus as regards the New World, as he was more learned than the horde of Spaniards and Portuguese which he left behind him; and last of all, this island, the Passaconaway, the home of the eagle, whose soaring ambition lifts him above the clouds, and, *mirabilc dictu,* just then the resting-place of the Colorado beetle, which crawling under our hammock was making his way to the East.

The gentle critic will here please note with what a graceful bound the historian's fancy leaps from the ridiculous into the sublime.

The neighboring shores of our river—did we not find them inhabited by civilized souls, men and women upon whose hearts was written the law of kindness, and whose hands were administrators of that law? Did we not find their homes the abode of sweet friendship and generous thoughts? Were we not happy in waiting four hundred years before starting on our voyage of discovery? Who dwelt upon our island then? Whose feet pressed the shores of either side of the river?

Was it worth while for a Columbus to sail to that sea-blown island, whose inhabitants were all barbarians? Or would it have been worth while then to have visited this valley of the Merrimac, where the forefathers of Passaconaway hunted squirrels and deer, fished for salmon and trout, and lounged in the shade, while their squaws hoed the corn and made the johnny-cake? And as for that matter, would it have been any more profitable for Mr. Passaconaway, senior, to have paddled his canoe over the other way and discovered the towers of Madrid and Lisbon, and attended one of their highly-civilized bull-fights?

Ah! the centuries have made some changes for the better since 1495. There is a law of progress, whatever the croakers say. The world growing worse? Does a peach grow worse when it hangs in the sun from August to September? In the sunshine of the centuries this bright, round world is ripening like a peach. Then shall not the centuries to come bring us the sweetness of still greater maturity? Wisely did the Laureate sing:—

"Not in vain the distance beckons. Forward, forward, let us range,
Let the great world spin forever down the ringing grooves of change,
Through the shadow of the globe we sweep into the younger day;
Better fifty years of Europe than a cycle of Cathay."

Better three score miles on the Merrimac, in the nineteenth century, than three thousand on the Atlantic in the fifteenth—better results, more significant discoveries! Shall we not felicitate ourselves on the change?

Really, the great mistake of the great explorer's life was in being born so many centuries ago. Could he have contented himself to wait until 1876, and then discovered our centennial exposition, how greatly more brilliant a name could he have left to posterity! And then, could he only have sailed up the Merrimac, and weighed anchor at the port of our island, how the view would have delighted his soul!

When some Edison invents a telegraph to transmit messages from the present back to the dark ages, we shall send Columbus a hint of the great gain he would have made by waiting a little.

Only a short look away from our tent was a barn that contained over a hundred tons of hay; and the owner and his sons, while fostering the interests of agriculture, were cultivating Christian dispositions and habits. Had they not learned the law of kindness? Were they not given to hospitality? True, the gentleman was not very full of professions, but he was fuller of alms-deeds. Did he not give his minister a load of hay? Men do not generally give hay by the cart-load to what they consider quack doctors. Was he not careful that his children should have a regular habit of attending church? Men are not usually solicitous that their children should be subjected to the treatment of quack doctors. He had some faith, which he had proved by his works. He would not wish his children to become the victims of a delusion. Was his faith small—smaller than a grain of mustard seed? That even may grow to a great tree. Let it have as careful nurture as he gives his growing crops, and his may yet become a giant's faith. Is it not as commendable and profitable to cultivate confidence as to cultivate corn or cabbages?

CHAPTER X. LOOKING TOWARD SUNRISE.

Perhaps you don't believe in early rising? Then again, perhaps you *do,* for other people—for those who like it. It is a good thing for those who need for its moral uses to see the sun creep slowly above the horizon. What better object-lesson could they have to prove that the day is growing brighter? For it is growing brighter. And there seems to be no more appropriate time than Sabbath morning to proclaim this Gospel of hope.

To our mind it was something to remember gratefully, that when the Sabbath brooded over our sweet island, the delightful and inspiring music of the bells of the city of Manchester came soothingly to our grove, suggesting thoughts of God, of love, of heaven.

Columbus heard no call to worship from the bells of San Salvador, or any neighboring island; nor would he have heard them then from the groves of Passaconaway.

It will be remembered that the great explorer did not discover the whole of America. It did not seem essential to our happiness, or to the completion of our plan, for us to discover the whole of the Merrimac. We had already found a delightful resting-place; and lulled to sweet content by the rippling river, the hum of bees, and the fragrance of the pines, we could hardly make ourselves believe that we should find a more enchanting spot anywhere this side the "islands of the blessed."

We rested there, enjoying the rich hours, and finding abundance of recreation under either cloudy or sunny skies. Our second Sunday found us in the glad and grateful possession of such good that without apparent effort our thoughts went upward, and busied themselves in a realm of sweetness and light.

Wendell and Parsons rowed to the Bedford side of the river and started on a two-mile walk to church. Serving as sentinel, we swung in our hammock, rejoicing in the sun, and imagining how Parson Goodhope would preach his sermon, *"Be of good cheer,"* to some people we know. It is an unpublished discourse, not copyrighted, and we violate no confidence in giving a few extracts.

The good book, my friends, is not a text-book for the grumbler; and the chapter is not yet written in which the disposition to snarl is spoken of as a Christian virtue. Such disposition, you may well believe, is better proof of a bad stomach than of a sound head or good heart.

Dyspepsia doubtless has its mission in the world. It is that of an avenger, not of a prophet. Dyspepsia is not the first qualification for a sound theologian. But if one wishes to set up as a croaker, it will go a good way toward the complete outfit.

You have heard with no little amusement, the pitiful whine of those dolorous souls, to whose jaundiced eyes and bilious imagination the race seems rapidly running to ruin. You have seen men whose golden age was far in the past, and to whose apprehension the present is an age of lead or pewter. And yet they will act as though they thought the age of pewter were perfect; for they uniformly oppose any movement that looks to improvement. They are sure to vote when the chairman calls for the "contrary minded."

You have had your laugh before now at the owl that was so conservative as to object to the new moon out of deference to the old one. And you will not be unwilling for the present hour to leave these owls to their lamentations, and with me join in thought the company of those more cheerful souls who stand in the dawn of the morning looking toward sunrise. You will find them good company, thoughtful as well as cheerful—cheerful because hopeful—hopeful because trustful, reliant upon Him whose beneficence is unbounded; who when He laid in the provisions for the race, by no means put all the choicest fruits in the top of the barrel.

If I supposed the most trustworthy being in the universe were like some contractors, that do not care to sell to a customer more than once, I should gaze upon the setting sun with infinite regret, and never think of looking for sunrise.

If it is not right to indulge in scorn for any of the human brotherhood, what is there left but pity for those so infirm of faith, as to believe only in themselves; or so full of conceit as to believe the world will lose track of its orbit as soon as they cease to guide it? What company can be worse than that of the bigot who expects that wisdom will die with him, who looks upon the world as a sucked orange, and who has been described in the choicest of classics, and with infinite pathos, as "having no hope, and without God in the world?" Believing in the Eternal Goodness, I rejoice with the children of Hope, that stand amid the hoary shadows of evil, glad in the conviction that these shadows are growing fainter, and are soon to vanish in the brightness of the better day. Let my song accord with that of the morning lark, joy incarnate, soaring above all clouds, and looking toward sunrise.

Do you ask how you may attain that health of body and soul which is so characteristic of the sons of Hope? Cultivate cheerfulness. Field says, be happy that you may be good. On the same principle, be cheerful that you may be well. Cheerfulness is to the man what sunshine is to the plant. Laughter is a means of grace to the body, as healthful as prayer to the soul. Life is flavored by it as fruit by the sun. What can supply the place of sunshine to the peach?

What is knowledge worth without the cheerfulness of wisdom? Of what avail is truth unless it be spoken in love? A jolly professor, using jolly in its best sense, as joyful, is the only fit man to teach theology. According to the true mythology, the presiding genius of Paradise is Joy. In her bright realm cheerfulness is one of the first conditions of citizenship. Be of good cheer, my friends, be of good cheer.

Have a purpose. A worthy purpose will speedily free the mind and spirit of the mumps and measles, dyspepsia and languor. Put your generation under some obligations to you—and your soul shall be buoyant with health. "The way to mend the bad world is to create the right one." Strive after higher things. Let not to-day shame to-morrow by its evil deed; but let it shame yesterday by its better deed! Do a good thing often enough to make it second nature. "Practice is nine-tenths," says Emerson. But don't make a machine of yourself. Maintain your liberty. Be generous to rivals; be liberal to opponents; fear not to learn from your enemy. Keep your temper in the battle. Be good-natured, whatever the provocation. The good-natured are the winning and successful souls.

Do not be afraid to think. If you have any brain use it. It was given for use. Dare, like Columbus, to tempt the ocean paths, and sail on to a boundless horizon. Do not starve your heart. Heart-wealth is better than gold. Look on all sides, north, south, east, west. Let him who will stick to his text; I shall the rather glance all around the horizon, while looking toward sunrise.

Keeping your heart pure, do not forget the purpose of your creation. I recall the case of one, a favored son of fortune, born as it seemed to be a prince among men; genius looked out through his eyes; fame twined her laurels around his brow; eloquence owned him for her son; beauty stood by his side. The Heaven that hovered around his infancy seemed long to bend over him in kindness. But, failing to guard with jealous care the portals of that inner temple where his manhood should have been held sacred, he fell, and the morn was draped in mourning. Of all the wrecks that have been the play, the scorn of the breakers, where is one so sad as the wreck of a stranded soul? Keep yourself pure. Soil not your spirit wings. Trust the Omnipotent. Cherish a worthy ambition. Neither whine nor dawdle.

Be true to yourself, remembering the soul's possibilities, and exulting in light immortal, you may sing peans to the rising sun.

The boys returned from church bringing a pleasant report; neighbor Foster favored them with a ride. They enjoyed the sermon; and spoke highly of the blackberries that grew in the graveyard. The berries formed a most cheering dessert for the Sunday meal. It would be quite an additional attraction if some other churches would have an abundance of blackberries in the adjoining yard. There is a period in the life of a boy when such a treat is very helpful in making up a favorable estimate of the Sabbath services. By all means let us be careful to cultivate a plenty of blackberries.

CHAPTER XI. SOLITUDE AND SOCIETY.

"How sweet, how passing sweet is solitude!
But grant me still a friend in my retreat
Whom I may whisper, Solitude is sweet."
—COWPER.

"There's nothing like being alone," said Patrick, "especially when ye have yer swate-heart with yer."

But this was not an original discovery with Patrick. Rather he was not alone in making the discovery. It is one of those peculiar discoveries of which there are a great many joint-authors. The first inhabitant of the original Eden thought he heard a voice announcing a similar doctrine. His report of it runs somehow like this: "It is not good that the man should be alone." There was at least one of the sons of Adam, who heard the same golden text re-echoing in his heart the Sunday night which we passed on Passaconaway. And the conviction of its truth was so strong within him that it appeared to be his reasonable duty to find a confirmation of the doctrine in some other heart, that he thought had begun to beat responsive with his own. It did not occur to him to look into the works of Lord Bacon for that confirmation. Though Bacon once said: "Whoever is delighted with solitude, is either a wild beast or a god." This Adam Jr. was no wild beast, though perhaps it would be slightly inaccurate to pronounce him an Apollo. He was not enough of a god to be delighted with solitude. And it did occur to him that one of the fair daughters of Eve lived in a neighboring farm-house. And it so happened that said farmhouse was not so many miles from our island home as to be out of the range of a good field-glass. Through the thoughtfulness of a kind friend who assisted in fitting us out, we had a very nice glass, and could look into the gardens and orchards of some very fine places, and almost into the windows of certain houses made attractive by gentle fingers and loving hearts. With a very little aid of the imagination we could see beautiful pictures, and hear the fragments of interesting and important conversations.

It also happened, that Sunday night, a little before dark, as the sun was kissing good-night to our island, and the moon, almost full, was brightening the western hills, and we were looking through the glass at the Uncanoonucks, that we discovered this Adam Jr. in his best attire crossing the fields toward the particular farm-house where dwelt the daughter of Eve from whom he had thought to obtain the confirmation of one of his heart's cherished beliefs.

It seems to be a characteristic of the human mind, that when we believe a thing very devoutly, we like to find and compare views with other sympathetic hearts that hold the same creed. Adam Jr. had a mind predisposed that way. And to his way of thinking there was no night as good as Sunday night for such religious conversation. It does seem peculiarly well adapted to this interchange of views.

So it has come to be a favorite night with the sons and daughters of the Puritans. Many people rather like to have it come round as often as once a week. Miss Eva was perhaps on the look-out for it. For strange as it may appear, just before our modern representative of Adam had come within sight of the house, she happened to think of a flower in the garden that she needed to decorate her hair; and stepping out to pick it, she happened also to linger a little under a vine where nature had constructed an arbor. Nature is at times very indulgent in the construction of lovers' bowers.

Our glass was not sufficiently powerful to detect the blush of surprise that covered her brow and cheek as Adam Jr. entered the gate and happened to know where to find her. But it revealed very distinctly the fact that it was not a bad place to find a being of such grace and gentleness. A natural arbor formed of trees and vines, with a flower garden on one side, and an orchard of choice fruits on the other, screened a little from any curious eyes that might be inclined to look out of the window, open to the smile of the setting sun, and the blessing of the rising moon, was a spot in itself of sufficient attractiveness to draw our hero and heroine away from any more lonely place, to enjoy a solitude there flavored with sweet society. By some singular foresight, chairs had been placed in the arbor, a little way, a suitable distance apart, just so that neither of them could well be lonesome. Adam Jr. expressed no regret at finding either the maiden or the chairs. Adam Sr. was probably not more delighted to find the queen of Eden when he awoke from his after-dinner nap, than our hero appeared to be to find Miss Eva in the arbor that Sunday eve. He may have been more surprised.

Neither was it an occasion of regret to us that we discovered their meeting and took note of the apparent ease and pleasure with which she offered him a chair.

And now it is far from painful to us to add a somewhat abbreviated report of the conversation that came to us by that invisible telephone which connects all lovers' bowers with the romancer's studio. It should be added that the report is not only abbreviated in its proportions, but is somewhat deficient in other particulars. No report can represent fully either an oration or conversation. It affords no clew to the intonations of voice, which sometimes add a charm difficult to represent in print. It docs not give the language of the eyes, which is also helpful to young people in understanding one another. This report leaves out a good deal that was spoken in an undertone—or whisper—too subtile to be easily transmitted by telephone.

And when the voices became indistinct, the lips spoke a language of their own; it would be as well perhaps to consider that lip-language confidential. Lovers sometimes make use of expressions not primarily designed for the historian's page. And at rare intervals gaps occur in the conversation, when silence seems golden. Our report will signally fail to convey the full eloquence of those intervals of silence; the reader must refer to his own experience for help to read what may be found between the lines. We can give only the prosy outline.

"Good evening, Miss Eva, how considerate in the moon to look in here so pleasantly on your favorite resort."

"Yes, indeed, Mr. Adam, and equally considerate in you to look in here about this time. Let me have the pleasure of giving you a chair."

Both take seats, not so far apart as to make the place seem chilly.

"May I ask, if you have with you the '*Confession of Faith*' that you were to read this evening?" inquired our hero, with the promptness of a man of business.

"O yes, you may ask; you like to ask questions, I believe."

"I do; why shouldn't I, of one so ready to answer? With your permission, I will ask if you have the paper?"

"Most certainly; did you ever know me to break a promise? You were to read yours first, you remember."

"I've been thinking it over; and concluded that we ought to have the same creed. You subscribe mine, or I yours. How can two walk together except they be agreed?"

"O, no, no; that will never do. Mine was not written for you. It is not sufficiently analytical for your philosophical mind. Mine contains but one article. You will more satisfactorily express your faith in five, ten, or fifteen articles."

"Fifteen? Why not fifty? Really, if we are to live in the same house, and eat at the same table, ought we not to have the same number of articles? How can we safely fellowship one another in the home, unless we have the same creed?"

"Will it not be really the same, even if not the same in form? If I believe in you, and you believe in me, is it necessary to particularize?"

"Well, let's see how they read. They may be so nearly alike, we can reduce them to one. May I see your paper, please?"

"After you, Mr. Adam; you were to read first. And we must stick to our agreement."

Adam Fr.'s Confession.

"1. I believe in Miss Eva Lilibest, as the woman best qualified to preside over my future home.

"2. I believe she has reached a sufficient age.

"3. I believe she has attained a sufficient size.

"4. I believe that she has possessed herself of sufficient knowledge—to begin with.

"5. I believe she is sufficiently domestic in her tastes and habits.

"6. I believe she can make good bread.

"7. I believe she can play the piano, *well*.

"8. I believe that her tongue has learned the law of kindness and discretion.

"9. I believe she is tasteful in her attire.

"10. I believe she has a liberal endowment of common-sense, enough for the family, and first-class talent for making a happy home."

"Thank you, Mr. Adam, for this clear expression of your beliefs. Without doubt you are sufficiently sound in the faith. Now listen to my heterodoxy. It is all summed up in one article."

"I believe that Mr. Adam Jr. is too provokingly good to be allowed to live alone; that he is the flower of his family, and that such a flower ought not to be permitted to blush unseen and waste its sweetness on the desert air."

Adam Jr. drew his chair a few inches closer to Miss Eva's. The telephone did not give distinctly the next remark. But the glass indicated a drawing together of heads, and a movement that looked as though he gave his sweetheart a kiss upon the forehead, in token of reverence for her superior intellect.

"They say your brother is going to be married about Thanksgiving time?"

"Perhaps."

"I don't see why that wouldn't be the best time for you to come over to our house."

"Why, Adam, the idea!"

"O the idea is all right. The only question is whether, as an abstract proposition, it commends itself to your judgment."

"I thought you were going to let me set the time."

"O yes you may set it next Thanksgiving, or sooner, if you prefer. Perhaps October would be better—say your birth-day?"

"O that's too soon. But don't let's talk about that now. Don't you know it's Sunday?"

"Yes; and I'm glad it is. If you will appoint some day in the week suitable for the consideration of this business I shall be only too happy to come over and hear you say next Thanksgiving. But I thought I would run over to-night and look over our creeds a little."

"I am glad you came. Do you find me sufficiently orthodox? We ought not to be married, you know, unless we are agreed in doctrine?"

"Well, for *substance* of doctrine you'll do, perhaps; but your creed lacks definiteness. A working creed requires to be more explicit."

"But if I do the work myself—I suppose I may let the creed rest. What work can a creed do, any way?"

"We are so well agreed in the fundamentals, so nearly one at heart, as I understand it, that we may postpone any further discussion till next Sunday night. Then, perhaps, we can reduce the two to one; one creed is enough for a single household."

The next Sunday night we were out of sight of Eva's bower. The telephone wires had not been laid to the place of our encampment. But in all probability their next attempts at creed-writing were perfectly satisfactory. They may have discovered during the week that hearts bound together by genuine love may analyze their faith as they please.

The reader who is curious about the result will find in the *Manchester Daily Union,* published a little after Thanksgiving, a notice of their marriage, which took place at the residence of the bride's father, just in time for the happy pair to drive to church that morning.

However it may be with a larger household of faith, it is not certain that any vital interests will suffer detriment, because they concluded to work together, even though inclined to construct their creeds upon different patterns.

When Columbus was cruising among the Islands of the Atlantic, he was told of two, inhabited one entirely by men, and the other by women.

Whether they belonged to some pre-Adamite race, and had not heard of Adam Jr.'s golden text, or Cowper's poetry; or, had discovered their fallacy, and agreed to live separately, Columbus did not ascertain. That was another of the discoveries which he failed to make.

The probable explanation is that they were unable to make their doctrinal statements agree and so could not dwell together in unity.

Our island was inhabited only by men, while we were on it; yet it is entirely accurate to state that our thoughts went sailing down river to a certain home we knew, even before our bark was set afloat to the music of homeward-bound. Not one of us, however, said a word about being home-sick.

Down the Merrimac.
Chapter XII. Homeward Bound.

We had discovered the New World, and rested in camp to congratulate ourselves, during a period of five days. We thought it would be well to leave the rest of the river for another trip. It is a mistake to undertake too much at once. That leaves nothing for the future, but to sit down Alexander-like and boo-hoo for other worlds. And it seemed impolitic to imitate all the great men at the same time.

We hadn't time to forget that when the great Christopher had finished discovering San Salvador and the adjacent islands, he concluded to forego the pleasure of finding the main land until another time; and he turned his little boat toward the east and set sail, without waiting for a letter from the reigning Queen, summoning him home.

We concluded not to wait for such a summons, and on the thirteenth of August, loaded our vessel and headed her down stream.

When Christopher started on his return trip he took with him nine Indians, thinking, it may be, to Christianize them by a sight of the bullfights of his native land. When we sailed from Passaconaway Island we could not find nine Indians that wanted to see the bull-fights at the oriental end of the Merrimac. And as there was no great demand for Indians down river, it seemed hardly worth while to wait until they should apply for passage.

We have not regretted our course in coming away without them. For we could not discover but that our Indian Summer was just as pleasant as though we had brought with us nine or "ten little Indian boys." Should any of our readers be curious to know the particular reasons for our neglect, the answer would be that our boat was not large enough to carry so many, and there were no Indians to bring. With a little assistance from their white neighbors, the Pennacooks had run out.

Christopher had a little larger boat; he had found a little larger island, where Indians were so plenty that nine would hardly be missed. He had determined to take back with him their gold; and it may have occurred to him that it was only fair to take the owners along too. And over and above all that, he left in their place forty-three of his own men that were hardly worth returning to their mother country. We considered our crew all worth taking home. And finally we did not wish to be too servile imitators of even the great Christopher.

Our boat had not drifted far on its downward course before we discovered that it was far easier sailing down stream than up.

It was, perhaps, not the first time that so remarkable a fact had been noted. Many of the greatest discoveries, like some great poems and stories, have several authors. They are like the Saxe Holm stories, that have been written by so many different women that it is difficult to determine who wrote them first.

Whether all the different authors of Hamlet and Macbeth have been found out yet, is known only to the critics.

It was easier going down the rapids, and over the falls even, than we could have imagined from any experience we had going up. And what was still more surprising, the falls were far more picturesque when viewed in retrospect, than when they afforded the prospect of hard work. This remark has no direct bearing on the labor question. Work abstractly considered has a charm of its own. Our question is for the artist- "Does the world always appear more beautiful to him who drifts with the current than to him who heroically stems the tide?"

However this may be, the vigorous pull on the oar develops strength, and strength is more to be coveted than delight—as manhood is more than pleasure. But the one who goes up and down river gains both.

We had our reward. We had gained the strength which the current gives to those who face it, and were permitted to return with the requisite health to enjoy the sweet pictures on either hand.

It was on our return trip that we rediscovered the fact that the Merrimac is a very crooked river. There was hardly a place where it ran long enough in one direction to give us a straight look of a mile ahead.

Here we run aground the problem of the ages, how to account for the crookedness of things. For surely some things appear too crooked even for the experts and detectives. They are like human nature, twisted in a way for which there seems to be no accounting. Attempts have been made by the world's sages to furnish a satisfactory solution, but with indifferent success. The poet has not withheld his hand.

"*In Adam's fall,*
We sinned all,"

is his lucid and concise explication of the vexed problem. It is perhaps safe to remark that neither the poetry nor the theology of the celebrated author seems to meet the wants of this cultured and regenerate age. Other poets have tried their hand, and some philosophers. But the latest conclusion in the matter seems to be to remit to posterity certain parts of the problem, not yet quite clear. And generally it would seem that problems which have come down to us from former ages, unsolved, had better be slipped along for the consideration of coming ages.

Yet it is well for every new philosopher to put in his oar. And while sailing down round some of the crookedest places in the river, not having much to do as sailors, we turned philosophers, and solved the secret of the river's winding ways.

We invented a very ancient tradition that when the bed of the river was laid out, the survey of its course was made by a drunken Irishman, who reeled about in such a jolly manner between the hills that he became everywhere known as "Merry Mack."

As he strolled round from city to city to get his bottle filled, he made a very crooked survey. And they named the river after him. That accounts for its running near so many cities, which it could not have done had Mack been sober enough to lay it out in a straight line to the Atlantic.

Sober Irishmen lay out water-courses in straight lines. Notable examples are found in certain ditches and canals. Whether the Merrimac would have been a more useful river, to have been laid out in a straight course from its source to the sea, is a question for future debating societies. Perhaps it would have been; but that would have been a bad arrangement for quite a number of the cities. It would have left Lowell and Lawrence far to the south. And what a sad thing it would have been for Lowell if the Merry Mack had not strayed in that direction! The tradition does not state whether Mack drank crooked whiskey, not whether he ever reformed. But it hints pretty strongly at the probable explanation of a great many crooked things.

It is by no means certain that it would sufficiently account for all the crookednesses of Wall Street; but it would go some ways toward an explanation. It would not be quite accurate to charge all the evil of the world upon crooked whiskey; nor would it entirely relieve the difficulty of the problem. For then some little boy would ask, who made the crooked whiskey? There would then be found a necessity for inventing another ancient tradition.

At the close of the day we found that we had rowed and drifted farther by several miles than we made in two days going up. We found a place for our camp so delightful that we could hardly help feeling a twinge of gratitude to the merry surveyor who had laid out the river's course so near our pine-crowned bluff. The climb, it is true, was a little severe. We were forcibly reminded that it costs an effort to get up in the world. And perhaps the genius is not yet born that can construct an elevator to lift imperfect mortals into heaven without an effort of their own. Even this wonderful age has not produced the mind to evolve a machine so wonderful as that.

"Nothing is got for nothing." Our effort of climbing, however, was abundantly rewarded. We gained a fine prospect, delicious air, seclusion, abundance of material for fire, a fine carpet, soft and dry, just the right place for an encampment.

Buckwheat was blooming on the Hudson shore, and sending out with every breeze sweet invitations to the bees to fill their hives with honey. At six o'clock our tent was up, the hammock swung, and we had an hour for supper, and to listen to birds and bees, and tinkling bells in the adjacent sheep-pasture. An hour for quiet observation and sweet meditation! Can any hour be more delightful than the closing hour of a beautiful summer day?

Swinging in our hammock we enjoyed sweet rest, cheered by music and soothed by the pines' soft lullaby. So cheered and soothed, there was nothing to prevent our drifting off into dreamland even more rapidly than the current had borne us to our restful haven.

Chapter XIII. A Pinch of Salt.

Early the next morning we cooked our oatmeal porridge, while basking in the warmth of a roaring camp-fire, and discussed the difference which a little salt will make, when it is left out. Our supply was exhausted, and it did not take us long to remember that "Salt is good." Our green corn was not so good but that it would have been better with a little salt. So much do the comforts and pleasures of life depend upon what seem to be the minor amenities, the small things that concern us! And our discomforts often depend upon very little things. The point of a needle, a mosquito's bill, the sting end of a bee, are very little things.

A trifle of the salt of kindness makes all the difference between the agreeable and the abominable. One kind word, or a pinch of salt with a little pudding around it, may save a starving man from suicide. Men do starve or commit suicide for want of that pinch of salt.

But it did not seem to be worth our while that morning, either to starve or drown ourselves just because we happened to be out of salt. It was too pleasant a morning, and the birds were singing in too merry a strain. It did not occur to us that it would be at all expedient to try in that way to punish a cold and heartless world for our own improvidence. It would not be expected of us. Nor could we see how that would at all mend matters. We thought, on the contrary, that rather than do that, we would go down to Nashua and buy some salt. We might have complained of the authorities of the town, or of the neighbors for allowing our provisions to run so low. We might have gone to the proprietor of the farm-house across the river and demanded that he divide his salt with us. Did not the early Christians have all things common? We are obliged, however, to confess that we did not think of this until after we had purchased a supply. Then, we had missed our opportunity. It was too late!

When we had finished our morning meal, we raised the question next whether to sail on. Wendell was of the opinion that we ought to stay over and enjoy our new home another day. Why be in haste to leave such attractive quarters? Parsons urged the thought that each day should bear us further on life's voyage. What aspiring soul can be satisfied to rest? A new home every new day—how much is implied in that!

Wendell was outvoted, and submitted cheerfully to move on. It seems to be the law of life that we move on, and grow on. Who would wish to remain an infant through eternity, the soul bound up in a nutshell? A chicken is not so foolish as to wish to get back into the egg.

"Build thee more stately mansions, O my soul!"

One about the size of the White House would perhaps answer every purpose. What a charm in the things that are new! What castles in Spain are more full of romance than the morning offers in the promise of a bewitching day? And the day did promise to be a glorious one; as if the weather-god having pouted and stormed, was endeavoring to regain favor by being extra good. So great was the change from the preceding week, that the weather itself seemed new. Yet with all the pleasures of the new and the strange, we found that when at night we encamped once more on our old ground, there was nothing in the new which reminded us of sweeter honey than the restful view of familiar places, and the winsome smile of well-known faces.

We found in the course of the afternoon some of the finest scenery on the river; some of which was overlooked when going up, or seen from some less favorable point. Some of the most charming of views are like certain human heads that need to be seen from the right angle to get the right impression of their beauty.

We met three boatmen going up in a canoe, who gave us pleasant greeting, and whose friendly interest drew out in their behalf our hearty good wishes for a prosperous voyage. How little is required to make men, perfect strangers, and ourselves also the happier for meeting.

The oaks and elms that had given us hospitality on our upward trip, waited to give us welcome; and we pitched our tent, with the leave of the owner, on the spot where we had spent our first Sabbath, and where we were to spend another, whose experiences were altogether so delightful as to deserve mention in another chapter. It was in Tyngsboro', on the east side of the river, at the upper end of Mr. Coburn's orchard. Having anchored our boat, and arranged our camp, and taken supper, we began to explore the land of Nod. It is verily a land of shadows; but that night the darkness was so dense, that we saw nothing. Our discoveries were so thoroughly forgotten that we had nothing to report but daybreak.

Thursday morning, the fifteenth, was specially noted for our early rising, and for the first bloody tragedy that occurred to us in the whole trip. Breakfasted at six, on fried lamb and boiled potatoes. We betray no confidence in pronouncing the cooking excellent; for we did it ourselves. After the breakfast dishes were washed, and the knives scoured, at eight o'clock and twenty minutes, the oak that bore up our hammock had its roots watered with human gore. Unconscious that any harm was about to befall him, Parsons was sitting in front of the tent, innocently whittling an innocent stick. He had never been to a whittling school, but had taken up the art of his own accord, and without special directions as to the use of a knife.

Suddenly, without apparent provocation, and without thinking specially about it, he thrust the shining blade of his knife into the fore-finger of his left hand. The gash was entirely too large; and the blood spilled was out of all proportion to the demands of the occasion. And to all appearances it was shed at far too cheap a rate. There was enough of it to have done honor to a greatly more important event.

In other respects the experiment seemed untimely. We were all sorry that he had not waited till after reaching home. But since the trial had been made, and the blood was flowing freely, and without any hesitation, it occurred to us that it might be as well to interrupt the stream in some way as to let the boy bleed to death. We knew that a pinch of salt is sometimes helpful in stanching the flow of blood. And we were fortunate in having renewed our supply. Parsons himself thought a rag would be of service; and on that account it would have been well to wait till we had reached home. We had forgotten to bring a rag-bag with us. We were over half a mile from any store. But the brave youth walked the entire distance and procured a quarter of a yard of cloth to bind up the disabled finger. With the simple reflection that blood less innocent had been shed on many a battlefield in a less worthy cause, we waited for the wound to heal. Time seems to be an important element in the curing of any wound, or the healing of any disease. The ills of earth may require a long time for their healing, but time, with the gracious help of Heaven, is doing his work.

After dinner the boys went to Tyng's pond, and I, with pencil and note book in hand, attempted the record of certain real and fanciful discoveries, actual and prospective, but so mixed that no account but the record itself can do justice to it. That the reader may not suffer an irretrievable loss, that is given in the succeeding chapter.

Chapter XIV. The New Earth.

The boys have gone a-fishing. I am the watchman, and abide by the stuff. By recreation and rest, I have become so far myself that I can speak in the first person. With returning strength the ego revives. Since there is more of me, I may indulge the ego with less impropriety. The man of two hundred avoirdupois may say "*I*" with an emphasis that is not permitted to a little man, unless he is equally big inside. Slim men should use the capital I with caution; but they may use it if they are careful about the underscoring.

While a man is not to think of himself more highly than he ought to think, he may nevertheless take the responsibility of being himself, and if sure of his health he may speak his mind; he may tell his experiences if they are delightful. Let the bilious and dyspeptic with doleful experiences be silent.

It is better to be mum than to croak. But when it is so easy to speak a pleasant word, why should any prefer to be mum? Let the well and strong, the healthy and happy prattle and babble, and laugh and sing. Joy is infectious, but it is not dangerous. To the new creature is revealed the new heavens and the new earth. To him there is liberty. Let him loose his tongue —it will run itself.

What a life-giver is rest! What a health giver the open air! I am beginning to feel that it is a luxury just to breathe. Never did a crust seem so certainly made of the finest of the wheat.

To sit in my tent and snap apple seeds at a fly is almost as enjoyable as was the hunt to the mighty Nimrod. But I do not sit in the tent very long at a time. The hammock takes precedence over the camp-stool. My hammock is swung between an elm and an oak, wedding beauty to strength by this easy yoke.

Swinging here, I can reconstruct ancient history, or dream of a world as real to me as was this continent to Columbus when he decided to find it. Looking up through the oak leaves that bend so gracefully to kiss the elm, I can weave my own romances and paint my heroes to suit me.

What do I care how Antony won Cleopatra, or what was the character of hero or heroine? In my new world the hero shall be the soul of honor, wise and true, brave and tender; and the heroine chaste as well as beautiful, fair as the morning, and inspired with the wisdom of love rather than the unwisdom of artifice. She shall speak not only fluently in six languages, but truthfully in all. She shall be ambitious, not only to rule others for their good, but chiefly so to rule herself that she shall never require the aid of an asp to terminate her career.

What do I care if Hannibal did vow eternal hostility to Rome, and harbor his malice for a lifetime? Must I make my heroes malicious in order to make them great? Nay, verily, the age is changed. The world is new. The hero of the nineteenth century is the great *lover,* not the great hater. His representative, sitting in the White House, sends out his messages, "with malice toward none, and charity for all." Kindly thoughts, beneficent purposes, fill his heart and mind, and his strong will is set to tasks of blessing.

The youth that flung himself into the river to rescue the drowning boy, shall sit for his portrait, and his picture shall be my Hannibal.

On the shores of this glorious river will I found my empire. Are they not mine by right of discovery? Does any one say they are already occupied, and that their inhabitants have a prior right? Did it signify that Columbus found America already inhabited? He discovered it all the same. He planted his colonies—and the result? Let the historian tell the story. Here it suffices me to give the history in advance of my own new world. This beautiful valley shall be the territory. The Merrimac shall be for it the river of life. And here shall dwell a people whose sons shall be heroes, brave, honorable men, mightier to conquer self than Alexander to conquer a world. Little will it matter five hundred years hence who now holds the title-deeds of these fruitful fields. Who owned them five hundred years ago? Who five thousand before that? What was their condition, and what their right to the soil? They slept with their fathers, and the world knoweth them no more. So shall the present generations pass, and a new people hold their title-deeds. I pitch my tent upon another's land by his leave; we strike hands in a friendly alliance; he brings my sons a present of fruit; I invoke a blessing upon his daughters. Together we visit the hill-tops, and stand upon his Mount Pisgah, looking northward, southward, eastward, westward, and heavenward. We behold sweet fields on either side of the river. I assure him that he has indeed a goodly heritage, that he dwells in a delightsome land. And I assure myself that my great-grand-children's great-grandchildren will hold it by reason of my discovery, and in their own right.

What concerns me most is that they be true men, brave and meek, strong and honorable, worthy to hold it, able to hold it, and nobly fulfil the purposes of being.

Is it not said, "The meek shall inherit the earth?" There shall be a survival of the fittest. And is it unreasonable to hope that coming generations will learn meekness of that lowly one, who is Lord of the whole earth? It is no mere fancy, but a reading of the law of progress by the eye of faith, which confidently declares that these beautiful residences that are so great an improvement upon the Indian's wigwam, shall, like them, give place to more elegant homes, with still more delightful surroundings. The new palaces shall re-echo with other voices and resound with other songs.

A higher civilization, a more refined culture, shall bless these homes, while a finer health and a loftier courage will add beauty and dignity to life. Beauty shall attend upon use; simplicity and veracity join hands, serving as the guardian angels of the home. Patience and moderation shall displace the hurry and worry which now fret the edges of life, and a serene faith shall hold to the promises of the Eternal.

And in those days the school-house shall be the temple of all useful learning; and the teacher an instructor in the science of right living. The pastor of the church shall be his colleague and chaplain, and the professor of moral science. The doctor shall be a salaried officer of the town, to lecture upon sanitary laws, and upon the means of preserving health. There shall be a gymnasium in every town, under the direction of a board of health, of which the doctor shall be chairman; and the grounds surrounding shall be fitted up as a public park.

The lawyer, instead of being an experimenter in the science of legal quarreling, shall be the expounder of political ethics, and lecturer upon political economy and morality. He shall give a public reading and explanation of such new statutes as concern the citizens of the town; and for keeping the people informed of their legal rights and duties, he shall be rewarded from the town treasury. And the people, prudent enough to refrain from litigation and disputation in matters of right, shall be wise enough to abstain from quarreling concerning the administration of the Gospel. They shall all belong to one church, or to churches bound together by Christian fellowship; and their religion shall be not only Christian in name, but Christian in spirit and purpose.

The church shall be administered upon principles as broad as the New Testament, which recognizes God as the Father of all, and all believers as brethren. It shall adapt its services to the needs of all, so as to hold and edify all the sons and daughters of the Lord Almighty.

There shall be one Lord, one faith, one baptism. There shall be no worldly-minded pastors, no contrary-minded deacons, no narrow minded partisans. But all, inspired with noble enthusiasms, with wise and fraternal consideration, with the generous purposes and beneficent spirit of their Master, shall illustrate to the world and to one another how Christians can love, forgive and help one another. Animated by loyalty to Christ rather than devotion to sect, they shall join hands in Christian work, and voices in Christian worship.

In that day the vocation of the editor shall be chiefly to publish delightful news. He will cheerfully be excused from exaggeration, and the manufacture of sensational items; as the public will have no taste for that style of fiction. He may publish receipts for preventing squashes from growing too large, and turnips from growing too tall. He may foretell the days when the sun will favor us with his smile; he may state when and where the lively pickerel will favor us with a bite; he may fill his columns with the record of generous and chivalric deeds, of fair and honest elections, of pure and profitable entertainments. There will be no murders, nor robberies, nor elopements to record, but happy marriages in high life, for all life will be high; and peaceful, natural deaths, for all deaths will be natural.

The children, learning early to swim, will not get drowned in the Merrimac, nor, any tributary waters. Thunder-storms will be so considerate as to dispense with the lightning that kills, or turn it over to some Edison, to be employed as a motor. Edge-tools will be endued with wisdom to cut only in the right times and places. Righteousness will be inscribed upon the threshing-machines and planing-mills; and circular saws will be hedged in with forethought. Tramps and diphtheria will be forbidden by law, and consumptions and fevers prohibited by fashion. No motives will remain for suicide, and none for scandal. Peace, plenty, and prosperity will fill the land; for the inhabitants will be so fascinated with honorable industries, and so devoted to minding their own business, that there will be no room for hard times. People will be so enamored of home, there will be little inclination to travel, unless it be by boat on the river; and husbands will be so in love with their wives, there will be no call for divorce.

The literature of that Eden? Well, it will consist in good part of prophetic romances concerning a still better time coming, and records of discoveries on the morning shore of the Millenium. There were never any such significant discoveries made by mortal eye as those we are permitted to make, by the eye of faith, in the new heavens and the new earth.

Ah, here come the boys from their fishing, as cool as two young philosophers. They have concluded that they went after huckleberries. In the dawn of the Millenium, fishing is considered a cruel sport; and it has seemed the part of wisdom to let the innocent pickerel that feasts on the smaller fish, have a little longer lease of life. This wisdom came late in the day, perhaps, and after an attempt to interview the pickerel; but wisdom had better come late than never come at all. Yet a riper wisdom is coming, though the world has waited long. It requires no prophetic gift to see that the world's best days are yet to come; only a little confidence in the truth, only a little exercise of hope. A healthful eye and a hopeful heart can see all manner of good in store for this beautiful valley. Let no well man be sorry that he was not born in the age of the Caesars, or of Columbus, or of Passaconaway. The canoe that brought Hannah Duston down the Merrimac sailed toward a sweeter civilization. We may hopefully spread our sails and hasten toward a more glorious future. There is no tax on hope, and no law against indulging it. The prayer of hope and of faith reads:—"Thy kingdom come. Thy will be done in *earth*, as it is in heaven!"

Chapter XV. Our Last Sunday.

After an ample breakfast of baked beans and brown bread, which is the average New Englander's most devotional diet, we discovered that we had too much time to get ready for church. Sunrise had came too early in the day for Sunday. We could not spend two hours upon our toilet, as we had left our Sunday attire at home.

When there is a large family to get ready it is very convenient to have sunrise early in the day.

It takes time to arrange all the fixings. In these days of modern culture, it is thought very desirable to have an elaborate church toilet. There may not be any such connection between aesthetics and religion as to make it essential for acceptable worship that the worshipper should have a thousand dollar jewel on the ring finger. But the sermons are usually so fine, so brilliant in the way of attractive points, not to say sensational, that the most devout hearer stands but a poor chance of attracting much attention unless dressed right in style.

As we did not have our "meeting clothes" with us, it did not seem to be our duty to compete with the more highly-favored residents and summer boarders. And it did not occur to us early enough in the day to excuse ourselves from attending church on the ground of indisposition. We were saved at least from one temptation, that of going late. Our morning devotions at the shrine of fashion were not so prolonged as to result in the disturbance of those whose feet were drawn early to the house of the Lord.

It is better, doubtless, to go to church late, when there is sufficient reason for it, than not to go at all. All civilized Christians ought to be as regular as possible in such matters. Church-going may be a mere habit with a great many; but it is a good habit. If a doctor is detained in the morning by a patient, and cannot get in until the sermon begins, he is excusable for being late. If a milkman's route is a little too long for his morning hours, he need not absent himself from the last half of the service because he cannot get in in time for the first half. But we are far from advising people generally to go late to church. It is not recorded that St. Peter ever went late; and if it were that would not make it our duty. There are advantages not to be overlooked in going early. If among the first, you can see whether the others enter suitably dressed, without having to consume the time of service in such inspection; that is, if the others are in suitable time. We went early to church that morning, and yet did not have the opportunity of reviewing some of the more important suits until the bell had ceased tolling. It is possible that a nicely fitting pair of new gloves, a "stunning" hat, or a pair of loud boots, will show off to better advantage just the last minute before the invocation, than at any earlier stage of the proceedings. Though some think it will do as well immediately after the invocation. The tramp of feet in the aisles during the voluntary affords a fine accompaniment to the organ, and helps put the organist, as well as the congregation, in a devotional spirit. We had been acquainted with a congregation further down river, that deserves commendation for being in time, and that, too, where the meeting is held forty-five minutes earlier in the morning, so we were prepared to believe that it is possible to get ready for church before eleven o'clock. It was a great surprise to us, therefore, to learn that the eloquent boots that passed up the aisle, just a little late, did not belong to a doctor or a milkman.

 The opening service was in admirable keeping with the cheerfulness of the day. It had been a good morning with the birds. In their morning offering it was not difficult to detect the flavor of glad hearts. So in the sanctuary gladness was expressed in song and prayer. It was good to be in such an atmosphere. There was an apparent heartiness and life in the worship which indicated that by far the greater portion had come to church for another purpose than just to see and be seen. The impression was that of devout Christian worship. Even those who came late and those who wore loud boots were well-behaved in the place of worship, and it is far from our thought to impute the sins of the boots to the persons who wore them. The sermon was not upon imputation, predestination, or reprobation. It set forth a Saviour, so human as to be in full sympathy with human nature, and so divine as to be able to save even sinful human nature.

The sermon—but it was not in our plan to remark upon the sermon. Only the Sermon on the Mount is above criticism; and that has not escaped. Had it been pronounced for the first time in some of our modern churches, it would be thought to savor too highly of good works, and to be lacking in the evangelical element. Perhaps there never was a sermon preached which was considered just right by everybody. But criticising sermons, even the Sermon on the Mount, is not necessarily the most profitable exercise of one's gift.

After the service we were invited to dine with the gentleman who owned our camping-ground; which we took as sufficient proof that he added to other virtues, this also, that he was "given to hospitality."

And a sweet hospitality it was, and hearty; giving us an opportunity for becoming acquainted with a rare and interesting character, a fine representative of one of the first families in the Merrimac valley—an old gentleman in the prime of life, over seventy in years, but less than fifty in spirits; a man with courage enough for a soldier, with information enough for an author, with voice enough for a general, and with dignity enough for a king. We had before been convinced of his generosity, and had grateful recollections of his visit to our camp with a present of melons and apples. And that Sunday's visit gave us some fresh glimpses of a heart both large and warm. Long may his extensive orchards continue to bear the finest varieties of apples yet invented; and his melon-patches furnish ample supply for two cities.

The Sabbath-school concert was the meeting of the day, judging by the attendance, and the effort made to interest the congregation. It helped not a little toward an answer to the question—how our churches are to hold their young people? Give them something to do in making the exercises attractive, and they will be interested in them.

The church was full. We saw no boys fishing by the discouraging river bank, while on our way.. There was something too attractive inside. Why not have a concert, or something as interesting and instructive, every Sabbath evening, and fill up our churches with youth and beauty whose delight in the sanctuary shall be expressed in songs of praise?

It is thought to be worth while for the pastor to prepare a sermon and a second sermon; but it is not so well worth while to have the second sermon as to have some service in which the children can have a part. Does it require some little trouble and effort? Perhaps the minister will say that it requires some effort to get up a sermon; but that is what he enjoys. The great question, however, is as to the comparative value of the different services to the congregation. The problem for minister and people is how to direct their work so as to profit the greatest number.

If only a small part of the congregation is interested in the second preaching service, it is a hint to devise some new arrangement. Jesus Christ is the same yesterday, and to-day, and forever; but there may still be an infinite variety of methods of presenting his truth, and so of presenting Him to the world.

The church that shall arrange its services so as to edify and refresh without wearying, the greatest number of souls possible for it to reach, is to be the church of the future. But we may safely leave the future generations to take care of the church of the future; it becomes us rather so to administer our trusts that the church of the present shall be the church of the people, of all the people, and so prove itself the church of the living God. Since He is the Father of all, why may not all be led to take delight in their Father's house, and through its ministrations be fitted for a place in the house not made with hands.

But this is not intended for a preaching service. It is not the chief end of man to hear sermons; nor always his chief delight. Something depends on the quality. It was once our privilege to be acquainted with an old gentleman, gone now, we trust, where there is no preaching, who wanted to hear sermons all the time; and yet he could take no delight in them unless very sound, and very dull. According to his judgment, a sermon was very sound that had a sufficient number of heads. He liked the thirteenthlies and sixteenthlies. Hardly any living preacher could suit him. Only the remembered homilies of some sainted divine could satisfy his critical taste.

But the cases are exceptional of men with intellects so vast as to require a continual stream of such preaching to keep them in good humor.

Chapter XVI. Music in the Air.

The night of the eighteenth, after a most delightful concert by the birds, we lay in our tent and dreamed of the most bewitching music. At seventeen minutes before twelve we were awakened very softly by the song of a bird that had been taking singing lessons of a frog. A new kind of music came stealing into our tent from the tree-tops above us. Your imagination will be the best guide in determining the quality of the tone. It did not sound like a robin. It did not resemble the barking of a dog. It was as much like a katy-did as the dulcet notes of the mosquito are like the voice of the cricket. It was not very loud; and yet a little louder than we should have chosen, had we been previously consulted. It was not by any means too cheerful. The music was written in the minor key; and gave the impression that the author was in a melancholy mood. That, however, was not the chief objection. It was untimely—too untimely to gain a patient hearing. It was too late for that night, and quite too early for the next morning. The other birds had all gone to roost, and were sweetly dreaming of a golden morrow; resting their voices for the morning concert. The katy-dids and katy didn'ts were cheerfully waiting a more suitable occasion for their little dispute, and were quietly gathering material for the next debate. Our musician was very inconsiderate. Really there was no call for his kind of music at that time of night. It was not given to meet any pressing want. We could not think of anything which we had done to deserve such a serenade. We reviewed all the sins that we had committed or omitted, and could think of none that merited such attention. Our conscience was all ready to go to sleep. The flesh was willing, and the spirit would cheerfully have acquiesced but for the disturbance.

It began to grow difficult to preserve our equanimity; patience was ceasing to be a virtue; for the strain was continuous, and quite too monotonous. It was provokingly monotonous. It was as humdrum and common-place as the stump speeches of a confirmed office-seeker, croaking "hard times, hard times, hard times; vote for me, vote for me, vote for me!"

How could an honest man sleep under such provocation? Yet the boys did sleep. Could it be accounted any proof of dishonesty on their part? Should we rouse them, and hold an indignation meeting in the dead of the night?

We endured it precisely one hour and a quarter, as nearly as you could measure it with a guessing rod; then rising deliberately we felt for the gun. Remembering, however, that it would not go off in the daytime without a good deal of coaxing, we concluded that a hatchet would be the surest weapon for dispatching that tree-toad. Then, if called to account for it, we could confess the deed in those immortal words—"I did it with my little hatchet." But in order to butcher a tree-toad successfully, it is necessary first to find him. We stepped softly yet resolutely out of the tent, and looked up wistfully into the tree. Our croaking songster did not seem to be embarrassed in the least. He sang away as though he enjoyed it. And yet, cowardly musician that he was, he would not come out and show his colors for love nor money. The night was serene. The moon looked down with provoking coolness, as though delighted with the serenity of the night. We wondered if the old man, her sole inhabitant, was in sympathy with our monotonous musician. He seemed so indifferent, so composed, as though sustained by the inward consciousness of approval from the man in the moon. He was thoroughly careless.

We had noted before that professional croakers are among the most careless of beings. They cannot condescend to pay any attention to what you say to them. Our tree-toad could not. Apparently, he did not hear our invitation to come down. The call may not have been couched in sufficiently flattering terms.

We threatened, but he heeded not. When we asked him just to show himself, he sang on as monotonously as ever. We looked for him; we looked again, we looked in vain, though we stretched our neck upward as far as possible to get a glimpse of him. Had the neck been six feet longer we might have seen him; but we didn't see him. We only heard him; and we kept on hearing him. When we asked him to stop for a rest, he seemed to feel like singing all the time. The case grew desperate, and we concluded not to butcher him, until we could find him. In sheer desperation we gave a whistle shrill enough to wake the seven sleepers, if they had been in hearing distance; and the tree-top was as silent as the grave. Felicitating ourselves upon the success of that whistle, we breathed a prayer of gratitude, piously recalled the commandment, "Thou shalt not kill," and went to bed.

Just as we were fairly covered in, our humdrum nightingale gave utterance to his conviction that we live in a free country, where the right of free song is as sacred as that of free speech. Not caring to debate so absurd a proposition at that unseasonable hour, but questioning seriously whether the right of free speech includes the privilege of croaking, we drifted off again into dreamland, where the tree-frog finds no welcome, and the croaker's voice is dumb.

Awoke next morning just too late to see one of the most delightful sunrises our eyes never beheld, but not too late to hear the concluding strains of a concert that would have done credit to the birds of the original Paradise.

While preparing and discussing the morning meal, we reflected upon the wisdom of that foreordination, that determined in the morning of creation that the tree-frog should exercise his gift at what we had thought an unseasonable hour.

It was for an example to the entire genus of croakers, who ought, in imitation of that night-bird, to tune up and let off their monotonous song after all respectable people, God's grateful ones, are abed, and sleeping the sleep of the cheerful and contented.

The doleful strain of the croaker is certainly more appropriate to the dark hours of midnight than to those bright hours which are gladdened by the sun. And if it were becoming in us to offer a word of counsel to the croaking tribe, it would run somewhat in this wise: "Go to the tree-frog, thou croaker, consider his hour, and carp away."

But do not think yourself anything great in the way of genius, because of any power to make the night hideous with your dolorous and monotonous note.

It does not require anything brilliant in the way of intellect, nor remarkable in the way of voice, nor very much culture, to make a first-class tree-toad. All that is essential is the disposition, and that can employ the most meagre talent.

Our last day in camp at Tyngsborough is not memorable for anything in the way of startling incident. Parsons went a-fishing once more; he did not catch a thirty-pound salmon, that would have worried himself and the fisherman almost into a fever before consenting to be taken ashore. Anything so exciting and thrilling as that would have marred the sweet quietude of the day exceedingly. Besides, the salmon of the Merrimac are too regardful of the legal enactments of the commonwealth to lend any countenance to their violation, by tempting susceptible fishermen to such unmanly sport. For can anything be thought more unmanly than for a self-respecting boy, or man even, to drop a line to a fish so much smaller than himself, and then chase him up and down river two or three hours for a favorable answer? To sit on the river bank, holding a long slender rod in one hand, and a nice little book which describes the bloody adventures of some mighty Nimrod, in the other hand, is altogether a more dignified proceeding; it saves the wear and tear of nerves, and is not so likely to wound the sensitive feelings of the salmon.

Father Coburn, under whose hospitable roof we had dined the day before, brought another melon and some green corn to our tent, and invited us to a stroll through his woodlot and pasture, where beautiful oaks, walnuts, and pines afforded refreshing shade. He led the way to the topmost peak of a hill, from which he showed us some pictures of the Merrimac—Nature's own—of the new iron bridge, of the old Tyng place, and other points of interest; while in conversation more delightful than the scenery, beautiful as that was, he gave us some charming glimpses of the mind of a philosopher and the heart of a friend. Long shall we remember gratefully that walk and talk with the old gentleman, whose devotion to Pomona has been equal to that of Vertumnus of old, and whose generous reward is abundant evidence of her favor. When he gave us our first taste of William's Favorite, a rich-flavored, high-colored summer apple, we could not help thinking that every gardener ought to have at least one tree, from which to treat his friends, after the Red Astrachan is gone, and before the Gravenstein is ready for eating. And we thought, moreover, that no one could take the pains which he has taken to raise choice fruit, still setting out trees in old age, without gaining a title to be considered a real benefactor.

And as we walked the length of his orchards and melon fields we wondered how our dejected night-bird could croak as if for dear life, "hard-times," in the very border of that loaded orchard?

When the question was referred to Wendell, the philosopher of our party, just then not quite so well up in etymology as in gymnastics, he replied, "That is all plain enough. To be compelled to overlook a field of unripe melons is enough to make any bird melancholic."

So we concluded that the croaker must be the sour fruit of an unripe age; and we slept in the hope that as the ages gain in ripeness, his tribe will become obsolete.

Chapter XVII. Home Again.

The Muse has tripped along the Merrimac with very nimble feet. And no wonder, if inspired for the journey by the genial song of our Merrimac Valley singer! It is enough to inspire any muse, or make any river beautiful to the eye of the light-hearted maid.

But never did the river seem more perfectly enchanting, than when, light of heart as a bird, our merry crew threw out sail, bade good-bye to our new friends, and sped away to greet the old. The elements conspired for our advantage; and nature's police did not interfere.

The current was strong and joyous. The wind was blessed with a helpful disposition. Both the river and breeze seemed glad that we were going the same way with them. It was socially exhilarating to go on together. The breeze was so overjoyed as almost to overdo it. It came near being so frolicsome as to be perilous. But our courage rose with the danger, and we keenly enjoyed our chase to keep up with the wind. Perhaps nothing is so sure to inspire one with courage as to give him a helping hand. Quickly were we borne by the encouraging elements, out of sight from our starting-place, down the roaring rapids, and past the Wickesauke Island, so swiftly that we had no time to invent any thrilling legends of hair-breadth escapes from our predecessors of the tomahawk period, who counted scalps by their cheerful camp-fires.

Gayly we bounded o'er the billows, which began to roll higher as the wind grew more daring, till it seemed that we almost flew into port at North Chelmsford, where we found the first familiar face we had seen for three weeks. It was the face of an old school-mate, whose eye, hand, and heart, were as full of welcome as his brainbasket of wit and wisdom.

The hour we spent in chatting over his trip to Palestine, and his prospective marriage, was all too short. Wishing him as much joy as it is proper for mortals to experience this side of heaven, we shoved our ship from shore, and sailed for the city of spindles and gubernatorial candidates.

A friend and disciple of the General, waiting with his team for a job, agreed to carry our ship across the city for a dollar; but before fulfilling the agreement it occurred to him to make an extra charge for the cargo. He did not say whether he had learned that trick in swate Ireland, or after coming to Lowell; he did not cite us to chapter and verse which encourages such a proceeding. We asked him if Thomas Talbot was not a man of his word? He mildly assented, and volunteered in addition the declaration that Mr. Talbot was "a very nice gentleman," but he was going to vote for "the Gineral." We did not undertake to argue the political question, but expended our logic in the endeavor to dissuade him from his purpose to inflate the charges. We could not agree with his candidate in all his little eccentricities, nor did we like to have the principle of inflation practised upon us, until after the election. We think the matter was made clear to his apprehension. He repented of his sinful device.

He was less than an hour in transferring us to the river below the city; and he bade us good-bye as respectfully as if his little scheme had been a success. We forgave him. We did not even lay it up against the "working-man's candidate." We did not believe that he was acting under the advice of a lawyer, when proposing to collect double charges. Lawyers are probably no more to blame for the faults of their admirers, than are ministers for the defects of their hearers. Some men are original enough in their sinning to do a good deal of it without the help of either lawyers or ministers.

We ran the rapids below the city without any great strain upon the oars, and stopped in a birch grove on a small island near the north side, to enjoy a small thunder-shower and take our mid-day meal. We have reversed the order though in our statement, for the shower kindly consented to wait until we had eaten our dinner. It was well; for so we could the better appreciate the shower, and pay it more attention. A thunder-shower always loses some of its attractiveness, when it undertakes to keep a hungry man from his dinner.

A delightful sail of an hour along precipitous banks brought us to the pines in Tewksbury, where on our upward trip we had spent the second night. We found a party from Lawrence fishing from their boats just opposite the harbor. They were hauling in the fish at the rate of about one every four hours. That would be a fourth of a fish to the hour.

The reader will be able to judge for himself about how high the excitement ran, and may possibly withstand the temptation to hasten thither to join in the fascinating sport.

The valiant knight of the hook and line, who at our previous visit had found a tempting array of fish in a convenient nook of the brook above, hastened up to see if they had changed their mind any with regard to coming ashore. He ascertained that they had at least changed their position. They were not to be found. Either they had acted upon the suggestion of some more expert fisherman, or in a fit of bashfulness betaken themselves to a more secluded nook. The disappointment was not great, and did not suggest the lamentation of the poet:

"'Twas ever thus from childhood's hour,
I've seen my fondest hopes decay;
I never loved a fish or flower,
But 'twas the first to glide away."

The Merrimac is very discreet. It does not undertake, by any such ignoble attractions as would be afforded by a multitude of the finny tribe, to divert the attention of the voyager from its charms as a river that has taken express pains to run along startlingly near to some of the most beautiful scenery out-of-doors. It is only farther down river that it ventures to offer the restful delight of fine landscapes, and the excitement of hauling in the monsters of the deep. Where it winds gracefully between the sweet banks of Haverhill and Bradford, Groveland, West Newbury and Merrimac, where the nimble sturgeon leap up for a sun-bath or an air-bath every few minutes, the excitement of fishing may be added to the other enchantments of nature. But even sturgeon fishing has its limitations in the way of attractiveness.

The next morning we built our last camp-fire, cooked our last breakfast of oat-meal and green corn, packed our dory for the last time, and rowed and sailed for Lawrence. There, while waiting for the attendant to lock us through into the canal, two young gentlemen from Lowell, in a shell, overtook us; and we had their company through the canal, and down river to a spot below Mitchell's falls, where we stopped for dinner. The run down the rapids, by the big flutter wheel, and over the falls, was very exhilarating and satisfactory.

As we turned round the great bend below the falls, and came near the lower rapids, where the river seemed sown with huge boulders, a great eagle, without waiting to obtain leave of absence, lifted himself from one of the rocks, and spurning the earth with his wings, soared heavenward; and after exploring the region of space in the vicinity of the sun, started in all probability for Eagle Island.

Judging from that specimen we concluded that the eagle is rather an unsocial bird. It is said that—
   "Birds of a feather
   Flock together."
We thought the eagle could not be one of that kind. He flew in a very solitary manner, and did not appear to flock together to any great extent, so long as our eye could follow him.

For social entertainments it is probable that the turkey excels the eagle. We have seen turkeys at social entertainments, which neither that nor any other eagle would be able to surpass. For purposes of oratory the eagle may be utilized; but for a regular diet the turkey is considered the better bird.

Whether it was in deference to the eagle as a high-flier that our fathers voted him the bird of our country, instead of the turkey, as was proposed; or did it with a view to keep the more toothsome bird out of politics to be reserved for society, history does not inform us. And, by the way, that is one of the most serious objections to history, that it fails to tell us just the things which we are the most curious to know. It is to be presumed that the fathers acted wisely in the matter, even though the present generation is not fully informed as to the wherefore. Possibly the turkey would cut quite as elegant a figure on our Bland dollars; but it might be difficult to get a supply of eagles for our Thanksgiving dinners.

As a matter of history it may here be recorded that upon our return home that night, we found no roast turkey nor fatted calf on the table awaiting our arrival. It was too late in the day for dinner; and too early in the season for Thanksgiving. It was two days earlier in the week than we were expected.

Instead of stopping to look for one or two more camping-places, as we had thought to do, we concluded to keep on our way and see if we could reach home that night, the more especially as the sky gave indications of a storm. A part of the way we had to row against the tide, and without the help of the wind. But neither wind nor tide could prevent our eager oarsmen, now skilled and toughened for work, from accomplishing their purpose.

At six o'clock we looked down the gap on the West Newbury side, where the river used to run before it turned to the left to run under Rock's Bridge. If it had not taken that turn travellers crossing the bridge would find themselves on the same side of the river they started from. And that would be perplexing.

At half-past seven we came in sight of Moulton's "Castellated Chateau," which adorns the heights opposite the Ferry

Village; and before eight we entered the mouth of the Powow, which we found had lost none of its kinks during our absence. At nine we were unloading at Boardman's Wharf. The row up the Powow was performed under the cover of a darkness so dense as not only to hide all the attractions and beauties of the surrounding scenery, but even to conceal the shores so effectually that we had to run aground several times to find out that the river had any banks.

Our run on the banks, however, was not a very serious affair for those institutions, or for ourselves. We came at length out of nature's darkness into the light of home, into the light of happy faces; and our gratitude was great, both that we had been able to leave a home so bright with the light of love, for a trip up river so full of blessing; and that we were able to return so strong to enjoy again the brightness and bliss, the rest and the labor, of such a home!

Index

A
Amesbury, Mass. 13, 14
Andover Hill 20

B
Bacon, Sir Francis (1561-1626) 39, 56
Bald Eagle 48, 91
Bedford, N.H. 52
Boardman's Wharf 93
Boston, Mass. 36
Boyd, Herbert Wendell, b. April 5. 1862 12
Boyd, Mary Ann (b. 1836) 11
Boyd, Willard Parsons, b. June 29, 1863 12
Bradford College 18
Bradford, Mass. 16, 91

C
Columbus, Mrs. (Filipa Moniz Perestrelo, 1455-14 10, 11, 15
Columbus, Christopher (1451-1506) 7, 10, 35, 38, 47, 48, 49, 51, 54, 62, 73, 77
Columbus, 'second' Mrs. (Beatriz Enríquez de Arana 11
Coos Falls 39
Cowper, William (1731-1800) 56, 62

D
Dracut, Mass. 22

E
Edison, Thomas 7

F
Ferry Village, Amesbury, Mass. 92

G
Goff's Falls, N.H. 43
Great Stone Dam, Lawrence, Mass. 21
Groveland, Mass. 16, 91

H
Haverhill, Mass. 16, 17, 47, 91
Hawkswood, Amesbury, Mass. 14
Heald, Louis 37, 38
Hudson, N.H. 37

I
Isabella I of Castile 10, 11

L
Lawrence Dam 21
Lawrence, Mass. 20, 23, 90, 91
Lowell, Mass. 91
Lowell Falls, Mass. 29
Lowell, Mass. 27, 29, 30, 31, 89

M
Merrimac, Mass. (city) 91
Merrimack, N.H. (city) 38
Methuen, Mass. 22
Mitchell's Falls, Haverhilll, Mass. 19, 91
Moore's Falls, Litchfield, N.H. 42
Moulton Castle, Newburyport 14, 92

N

Nashua, N.H. 37
Nashua River 37
Naticook Island, Merrimack, N.H. 40
Newburyport, Mass. 14
North Andover, Mass. 20
North Chelmsford, Mass. 30, 88

P

Passaconaway, (c1580-c1673) 48
Passaconaway Island 45, 48, 51, 63
Pipestave Hill, West Newbury, Mass. 14
Powow River, Amesbury, Mass. 12, 13, 93

R

Reed's Ferry, Merrimack, N.H. 40
Reed's Island, Merrimack, N.H. 40
Rock's Bridge, Haverhill/West Newbury, Mass. 16, 92

S

Salisbury Point, Amesbury, Mass. 16
Salisbury Woollen Mills, Amesbury, Mass. 12
San Salvador Island, the Bahamas 47
Shawsheen River, North Andover, Mass. 20
Short's Falls, Manchester, N.H. 44
Souhegan River, Merrimack, N.H. 40
Spofford, Harriet Prescott (1835-1921) 14
Stackpole St., Lowell, Mass. 29

T

Tewksbury, Mass. 22, 90
Tyngsborough, Mass. 36

W

Washington, Geo. 37
West Newbury Church 14
West Newbury, Mass. 16, 91, 92
Wickesauke Island 30, 31, 88

Author's Biography

Pliny Steele Boyd, was born in Griegsville, New York, May 18, 1836. A Congregational clergyman, he wrote much for religious periodicals and published two books.

After graduating of Oberlin College in 1860, Rev. Boyd studied Theology at Andover Theological Seminary from 1862 to 1865. He was in the service of the United States Christian Commission in 1865-66, and was ordained and installed as pastor of the Congregational church at Shelburne Falls, in 1867. He was made pastor of the Congregational church at Ridgefield, Connecticut, in 1869.

In September 1860, Boyd had married Mary Jane Allen (b. Sept. 16th, 1836,) the daughter of Rev. Ralph Willard Allen and Mary Jones Tower of Southbridge, Mass. The couple has six children, all boys: Herbert Wendell, b. at Hingham on April 5. 1862, Willard Parsons, b. June 29, 1863, Edward Steele b. Shelburne Falls, September 8, 1867 (Amesbury High School in the class of 1885), Maurice Chester, b. Ridgefield. Conn., June 16. 1869, Charles Allen, b. Amesbury, July 23, 1874 and Pliny Arthur, b. Amesbury, March 10, 1876. She died on December 2nd, 1905 at Bloomfield, N.J.

In 1871, Boyd was called to Amesbury, Mass. as pastor of the Union Congregational Church, where the family lived until 1886. It was in August of 1878, when Boyd and his sons Wendell and Parsons took their month long sojourn up the Merrimac River from Powow River in Amesbury, Mass. to Passaconnaway Island in New Hampshire and back again.

In 1886, Rev. Boyd, settled at Granby, Massachusetts, where he remained until he died in December 6. 1887.

www.ingramcontent.com/pod-product-compliance
Lightning Source LLC
Chambersburg PA
CBHW031411040426
42444CB00005B/523